Elisha Mulford

The Republic of God

An Institute of Theology

Elisha Mulford

The Republic of God
An Institute of Theology

ISBN/EAN: 9783743382176

Manufactured in Europe, USA, Canada, Australia, Japa

Cover: Foto ©Lupo / pixelio.de

Manufactured and distributed by brebook publishing software (www.brebook.com)

Elisha Mulford

The Republic of God

THE

REPUBLIC OF GOD.

An Institute of Theology.

BY

ELISHA MULFORD, LL. D.

FOURTH EDITION.

BOSTON:
HOUGHTON, MIFFLIN AND COMPANY.
The Riverside Press, Cambridge.
1882.

The Riverside Press, Cambridge:
Stereotyped and Printed by H. O. Houghton & Co.

TO MY CHILDREN.

CONTENTS.

CHAPTER I.

CHAPTER II.

** The references to the Scriptures are in a few instances nec
essarily a paraphrase, simply conveying the substance; but these
may be readily verified, and in some instances another translation·
has been given, but only when sustained by the most critical author-
ities.

MONTROSE, SUSQUEHANNA COUNTY, PENN.

THE REPUBLIC OF GOD.

CHAPTER I.

THE BEING OF GOD.

THE being of God is the precedent and the postulate of the thought of God. It is the ground in man of his conscious life. From the beginning, and with the growth of the human consciousness, there is the consciousness of the being of God, and of a relation to God.

Man is conscious of the being of the external world, and lives and acts in this consciousness, and the being of the external world so comes to be apprehended by him. And, further, man is conscious of the being of God, and lives and acts in this consciousness, and the reality of the being of God so comes to him.

We cannot deduce the being of God from the existence of the world, nor the eternal from the temporal, nor the infinite from the finite; and yet the temporal has its ground in the eternal, and

1

the finite in the infinite. The eternal is not the continuation of the temporal, nor the infinite the extension of the finite, and God is not the sequence nor the limitation of the world.

In this process of the consciousness of the being of God, man does not start from the finite existence which is within the conditions of space and time, — that which consequently is placed.[1] Being is of itself, in finite conditions, a vacant phase of thought. It is not that we have to ask its application, as derived from the finite existences, to God.

The notion of God is derivative from the being of God. It is not necessary to supplement the notion of God with the empty category of being as derived from finite conditions.[2]

---

[1] "We must find something like God before we reach God, or we shall not in our thoughts attain unto him." (Bascom, *Philosophy of Religion*, p. 74.) It is necessarily the reverse of this. We know God, and then we find that which in a higher or lower measure is like him.

[2] Kant (*Werke*, vol. i. p. 90) does not prove the difference between being and notion. It is assumed in a popular way, but it is a phase of thought which applies only to imperfect or incomplete things.

Thus, in society the state advances in its normal process into the realization of the idea of the state, and the course of the physical world may be a development, after its germinal or radical type, through the succession of its forms. But this process does not pertain to the being of God. He is not the sequence of an evolution, though his manifestation may be through the process of an evolution. God is the perfect being, and incompleteness does not attach to him.

If Kant's postulate is correct we can know nothing of God ; we can make up various notions about God, but that is not to say that

The being of God is not an attribute which is to be appended to some abstract notion of reality, or of the sum of all realities, or to the notion of perfection, and if it were in this constructive method to be thus apprehended, it would have the place of an attribute and not of the subject.

Thus it is not necessary to the knowledge of the being of God to assume that it is one among several objects of immediate intuition; nor that it is a requisition of the emotions, — the requirement that there shall be placed before them the highest end; nor that it is arrived at, as a conclusion, through the formulas of logic.

The knowledge of God thenceforth, in this process of consciousness, comes through experience. It is the experience of the individual and the family and the nation in the life of humanity.

The being of God is the primal truth. It is primitive in human thought: there is nothing before it nor apart from it, from which it is to be derived. Thus the being of God has not its foundation in the life of humanity, but humanity has its foundation in the life of God. Theology has not its ground in psychology.

The idea of God is in and with and through the

these notions are so, nor is the existence of God implied by them. See Hegel's *Philosophie der Religion*, vol. ii. p. 214.

being of God. The idea and the being of God are one. In Him is the oneness of the ideal and the real. It is only in and from the being of God that we discern the infinite and the eternal in their realization.[1]

The infinite is not subject to the conditions of the finite, nor the eternal to the conditions of the temporal. In the physical process we can attain only to the negative infinite, the temporal and spatial infinite, that is, the quantitative infinite. The imagination is dissatisfied with this, and passes beyond it, but only through its ideal qualities. That the conditions and conclusions of thought are not the same in the finite — the temporal and spatial — is no argument against this position.[2]

---

[1] It has been said of one form of the ontological argument, " It infers the being of God from the ideal necessity of being to the conception of infinite attributes. It thus accepts a connection of ideas as a proof of facts." (Bascom, *Philosophy of Religion*, p. 60.) This is critical of a merely formal process of thought that assumes " infinite attributes," and then assumes " being " also, as an attribute that is attached to them through a " connection of ideas." But in the ontological argument strictly there is no " connection of ideas " assumed. For the idea and the being of God are one, and it is only in and from the being of God that we discern what are called his " infinite attributes."

Again, it is not from the notion of a perfect being — " the conception of infinite attributes " — that the reality of being is deduced, for the argument does not assume an attribute of perfection to which existence is to be appended, and if existence be an attribute or perfection of God it must take the place of an attribute and not of the subject.

[2] The ontological argument of S. Anselm, as it has been represented in the interpretation of a school of formal logic, has for its postu-

There is no demonstration of the being of God. It is itself the principle of demonstration. In every mode of demonstration whose object is to arrive at it, it is assumed. It can form no term in the formulas of logic. It is not a truth which is to be counted among the achievements of human thought. There can be no demonstration of the being of God by man: there may be the manifestation of God to man.

The name of God is that name which passes into the common forms of thought. In its derivation it may have an ethical significance. It has

late the thought of a perfect being — a being than which none greater can be conceived, and then it attaches the attribute of being to the thought as necessary to its perfection — as that lacking which it would lack perfection.

But S. Anselm's argument strictly is as follows: God is something than which nothing greater can be conceived: but that cannot be in the intellect alone. If it were only a thought it might be conceived as existing, and that would be something greater, therefore existence is necessarily implied in it.

The representation of S. Anselm's argument by a school of formal logic, as Hegel says, implies an antithesis of thought and being. But S. Anselm compares two modes of conceiving the perfect being, that which conceives him as a mere abstraction, simply an object of thought, and that which conceives him as really existing, and he maintains that so long as God is conceived only as an object of thought — that is, as a product of the human mind — we do not conceive that than which nothing greater can be conceived, in which the definition of God consists. Thus Hegel says: "The profound thought which the argument involves has acquired a false and shallow aspect from being forced into the form of a conclusion of the understanding." See Hegel's *Philosophie der Religion*, vol. ii. p. 541; Hedge's *Ways of the Spirit*, p. 176.

a definite place in the language and literature of English-speaking men. The substitution for it of forms which denote some special phase of thought is an indication of weakness. These terms are often the sequence of an argument for the being of God. They often have the stamp of certain schools upon them. Thus the term "supreme being" implies the notion of being which is relatively more and higher than other forms of being.[1] It has no content, and implies only the empty abstraction of indeterminate, but yet relative, being. It has not a certain strength which is in the term "central being," as in Dante's phrase, "truth deep as the centre." The term "first cause" indicates only one, if it be counted the first, in the sequence of the forces of the world, and these forces often apparently move through forms advancing from less to greater. The term "providence" indicates a notion as to the determination of these forces, in what it further defines as a special or general way toward a certain end. These phrases were widely prevalent in the style of the last century. The terms "the absolute," which is characteristic of the Greek thought, and

[1] This phrase is used by Edwards, and becomes the basis of his theory of the nature of virtue, the love of the more and higher over the less and lower being, which has thus only a quantitative character. An ethical content is imported from some incidental reference, or some other writings of Edwards, but it is lacking in his theory of virtue. The same conception is carried, in another form, into the sovereignty of God, which is thus a bare sovereignty, — the starker stronger force.

" the infinite " and " the eternal," are more significant and comprehensive than the preceding, and
denote the high service of philosophy. Thus the
terms " the .word," or " the divine word," or " the
eternal word," indicate a truth of the deepest significance, while yet they retain, in their literal
form, the trace of certain schools and epochs, and
recall their relation to these in the history of philosophy.

The evidence of the being of God from the
being and condition of the physical world is not
to be traced in the common lines of thought in
which this argument is presented. The argument
which has this inference for its object has been
called, in the term of the schools, the cosmological
argument.

A special form of this argument is based upon
the notion of causality. The process of causality
appears in the physical process. But causality
here is the transference of force. And the cause
is always contained in the effect, and the effect
measures the cause from which it proceeds. We
cannot transcend the effect as we pass through
the being and condition of the physical world to
its cause. And the law of causality, which is adduced, itself forbids a stop in its numeric preces-
sion, which is to be designated as a first cause, itself having no precedent. This would subvert the
very principle which is assumed as the foundation

of the whole structure. And the cause, which is physical, can be invested with no other qualities, for instance, with no intellectual or moral quality which is not in the effect.

The argument aims to transcend the physical process by the application of a law in which that process and the persistence of that process are constantly implied. There is no recession through which we pass, in the process of the physical world with its finite changes, to the being of God.[1]

But the mind of man is left unsatisfied. It is still led to follow that which is beyond and still beyond.

There is an argument derived from the being and condition of the physical world, on the ground that the universe bears traces of intelligence, — of thought and will. This has been called the argument from design, — the teleological argument.

This argument in one form rests on an analogy between the physical process and the works of man; as when from the design, in the tools, the buildings, and the streets, we infer a designer of them. This strictly would involve by way of analogy, man as an animal, and then, also, other animals of certain lower forms, as the bird that builds a nest, and the insect that makes a cell.

But while man as involved in this physical pro-

---

[1] " The universe lies forever back of the universe." (Bascom, *Philosophy of Religion*, p. 41.)

cess has intelligence, this product cannot carry us beyond the process itself in which it exists. The indications of intelligence, moreover, are not limited to conscious action, but they appear in unconscious movements, as in the structural uses and functions of the human body. The argument, instead of showing thought as antecedent, shows it as pervading the whole, and in a process whose apparent mode of operation is that of necessity.[1]

And there are in the works of man other and higher qualities than those which appear in the physical process. The music of the storm, of the sweep of the surges of the ocean, is not so impressive as that of great orchestras. The tree that sways in the wind has no tones to compare with those that are brought out by the viol and the flute. It is the human element that gives to the landscape its deepest attraction.

It is said in the old phrase, that in the physical process there is an adaptation of means to an end. But if this phrase be allowed an application to the physical process it is only the evidence of intelligence, and the degree of intelligence is in the completeness of the adaptation of the means to the end. This adaptation is also modified by the relative imperfection of the physical process, which

[1] "The being that emerges under the teleological proof is the universe itself, as an organic unconscious conscious being. The teleological argument breaks down, not because it does not reach intelligence, but because it includes it, and includes it among necessary forces." (Bascom, *Philosophy of Religion*, p. 68.)

appears in the fact, for instance, that in every class or species the individuals are comparatively few that attain to the normal type. In any evolution of forms the variations are but slowly effected, and the forms displaced still in some instances remain, and in individuals recur when all use for them is gone. This led Hegel to say, that in the physical process the idea is slowly and with difficulty developed, and in its processes there are many divergences, as if nature were not always very clear in her own intent. There is, however, in the physical process only the evidence of adaptation to the circumjacent condition, and not to a determinate end. And this adaptation of means to an end, or of the individual to the environment, bears, in the physical process, the evidence of no moral quality.[1] In the physical process, the beak

[1] The witches in Macbeth, that are gathered on the lonely heath in "fog and foul air," stand very near to nature. They begin their strain of dolor, with

"Fair is foul, and foul is fair,"

in her indifference. They gather at hand, to throw into their seething cauldron,

"Eye of newt and toe of frog,
Wool of bat and tongue of dog,
Adder's fork, and blind-worm's sting."

Macbeth calls to them in the same moral indifference, out of the course of nature,

"Though the yesty waves
Confound and swallow navigation up;
Though bladed corn be lodged and trees blown down;
Though castles topple on their warders' heads;
Though palaces and pyramids do slope
Their heads to their foundations; though the treasure

and talons of the hawk are adapted to clutch its prey with almost no pause in its swift flight. The flower is formed for the distillation of poison, and plants which are useful are so mimicked by those which are hurtful that only constant scrutiny, after fatal experiences, can detect the difference. The toadstool grows close by the mushroom. The fruit which the tempter found already growing was fair to the eye. Hegel says, the earth declares the goodness of God, and that his goodness appears in this adaptation of means to an end, but it is only when this physical process is considered with reference to that which is beyond it, to an end which it brings not within our observation, that these words are justified.

The conditions of this process are those of conflict, a struggle for existence, it is

" The rack of this tough world,"

and one form passes beyond another form by sur-

> Of nature's germens tumble all together,
> Even till destruction sicken; answer me."
> *Macbeth*, Act IV., Scene 1.

Man, as involved in the physical process, and as an object of physical science, in a school which holds these limitations, has no other dignity than attaches to any other animal. His cunning may outmatch the fox, but it has no other quality; his powers of digestion are the same as those of the rat; the fly does copulate as he; the dog may quarrel with him for his food; the shark may prey upon him, as he on the shark, and with advantage when it finds him in its own element; he learns the conditions of physical existence from the anatomy of other animals; vegetable and animal parasites grow and feed on him; his life as involved in the physical process has no other dignity, it is of the earth, earthy.

vival. There are in nature elements of subsist-
ence for production and for destruction. One
race to subsist must prey with ravin upon another race.[1] There is the adaptation of the wing of
the crow and of the tooth of the shark. There is
a strange intermingling in the poison that fills the
chalice of the most beautiful flower, the malaria
that is borne upon the softest airs, the color that
gleams resplendently in the sinuous folds of the
serpent. There is the fair light that illumines the
dawn and empurples the evening, but throws its
radiance over mists and exhalations. There are
smooth waters that bear the reflection of the
clouds which hold the tempest, and are changed
with the clouds which burst over them into the
rage of cruel seas. The tides rise and fall with
almost changeless precision, but they are swept by
the storm that marks their lines with wreck. By
the cleft and broken strata of the rocks, one may
still seem to hear

" the sea rehearse
Its ancient song of chaos.'

[1] There is a school which assumes the identity of God with the
physical process of the world, or with what it calls " the nature of
things." It identifies God actually with the course of physical nature, with the nature of things in the current physical condition of
the world. Then that which is apparently inexorable and cruel is
directly ascribed to him. That which in its transient course is dark
is ascribed to Him *in whom is light and no darkness.* But it would not
be true even to assert the identity of man thus with the nature of
things. It would be a degradation of man in whom is the life of the
spirit.

There is in nature that which is beautiful and that which is fantastic and monstrous. These aspects of nature become more apparent in tropical countries, where there is a stronger movement of the impulse, the passion of nature, with more impetuous energies. Thus in India there are more images and shrines of supplication to Siva the destroyer, than to Brahma the creator, and Vishnu the preserver.

For individuals and races this physical process is one of successive survivals followed by cessations of existence. There is the extinction in this succession of individuals and races, and whatever may be the effect of means, or of conformance to that which is contingent, death is the end. The research of geology indicates the mutations of cold and heat, through long epochs and over vast continents, which would bring a termination to every form of life within our knowledge. We may admit the strength of the force working in material moulds, and the persistence of the movement in this evolution which slowly modifies itself with its environment, and maintains unbroken adhesion to its types, but there is no evidence that that which is lower is always displaced by that which is higher, nor that any displacement is permanent.[1]

---

[1] It has been truly said that the Darwinian is the derivative, not the development hypothesis. It is not always from the lower to the higher, nor in that sense does the fittest survive. Strictly it fur-

These indications of ugliness, of rapacity, of cruelty in nature, it is said, are on the whole not to be noticed. But they are there. They pervade the whole, and are involved in the whole process of the physical world. They have in certain lands and ages a potency that overmasters the imagination and fills it with images of dread, and so they mould the thoughts of men, as they have found expression in literature and art. It is said that a balance is to be struck between the fair and foul, the beneficent and cruel; but this, however the balance swayed, would only indicate, and in that exact degree, a mixed quality of indifferent good and evil in the intelligence which formed the world, or appears in the evolution of its forms.[1]

nishes evidence only of the survival of the one best adapted to the situation, nor does it furnish evidence that the situation materially improves; on the contrary there are indications that would show the recurrence at long, and it may be, periodic intervals, of ages of gradual extinction, as the geological ages of ice. And while, in the physical process from and through geological periods, there has been in physical forms apparently an increase in the complexity of organization, there has been a diminution of physical force and bulk.

[1] This argument in one form is based on the order in nature. Janet says "the order supposes an end, and the very principle of order is the end." (*Final Causes*, p. 215.) The doctrine of final causes has its justification in philosophy. But in the physical process there is no evidence for a final cause and end, nor against it, and no evidence of the character of that end. There are around us only the circling suns — *flamentia mœnia mundi*. This argument identifies the current, the existent process with order, and then assumes that this order, which is the existent process, is the final cause

There is in the process of the physical world no moral quality, no manifestation of the will, as in the life of the spirit; it is as Hegel says, "the other" of the spirit: it is only elevated and informed with a moral attainment through the mediation of the spirit.

There is in the physical process no manifestation of freedom, nor is it in man, as he is involved in the physical process. There is in it no trace of personality.

There is in nature no strain of sympathy that breaks its indifference, no love interrupts its inexorable course. No appeal can stay its falling rocks. No entreaty can restrain its beating waves. It has no power to help man in his calamity. It does not turn to avert his injury, nor to mitigate his pain. The clown says to the old man in the storm —

> "Here 's a night that pities
> Neither wise men nor fools."

It is only in a figurative way that there is any declaration of a moral quality in the physical process. It is simply without the moral.

and end. This is simply a change of phrases, while the actualization is the same.

The end of this order for individuals and races is death, and the inference is that this order is continuous. And order is not so profound a conception as life, and, in the physical process, the final cause and end of life is death. The adaptation to a circumjacent condition may be a degradation with the extinction of higher energies. This process is not in any moment in itself what Renan calls it, "an eternal order," nor the end in nature.

These facts must be brought into a more profound synthesis, and it is the merit of the cosmological argument, however crude and deficient, that it has made an effort toward this.

In this synthesis, the oneness of the life of man in its physical process with the physical process of the world, the physical conditions of the attainment of the ethical life; the recognition of the finiteness of the finite, the transience of the transient in the world, through the negation of the finite, and the fulfillment of the finite in its life in the infinite; and the necessity of reconciliation for the satisfaction of the spirit, — these are brought to their resolution in thought. These are postulates of this synthesis that have found expression in the most profound and enduring forms of the religion and the philosophy of the world.

It is not from the physical process with its finite conditions that there is the evidence of the being of God. There is no discovery of him in the furthest research into the elements of the suns, no traces of him in the strata of the rocks, there is no finding of him at the roots of the tree, or in the dust of the stars.[1]

[1] "It is indeed not on the finite ground occupied by the physical sciences that we can expect to meet the indwelling presence of the infinite, and thus Lalande has said, he had swept the whole heavens with his glass and seen no God." (Hegel, *Encyklopadie*, vol. i. p. 128.)

"Though we allow that this argument from design and therefore

The thought of man passes through the physical process to the apprehension, through the succession of its phenomena, of the universal, but this is only by its ideal quality.

Thus the transient recalls to the mind that which is not itself transient, and is not subject to transient conditions. The flower fades while the maiden gazes upon it, but with it beauty itself does not fade : that is imperishable. But nature in herself does not intimate this. The beauty that fades with the fading flower is cast aside by her with weeds and worn-out faces.

There is in the physical process a necessity, and there are relations of sequence, from which may be derived the inference of natural laws, a law of nature. This necessity is, however, not inconsistent with the attainment of freedom, although freedom has not its manifestation or realization in it. It always subsists as an element in freedom, and may be taken up and transmuted into freedom. There is, whatever may be the extent of its range, a mode of action or a law of the physical process by which that which is lower may be carried on to that which is higher, and retained as a moment in the higher.[1] Thus man,

a designer, furnishes an explanation of physical phenomena, the fact of an infinite and perfect being does not follow." (Hedge, *Way, of the Spirit,* p. 161.)

[1] " In the gradual series of earthly existences the law holds good that the higher essence takes up into it the character of the lower as a moment." (Ueberweg, *History of Logical Doctrines,* p. 93.)

who is representative of the higher forms of life, is connected with the lowest forms, and subject to the incident of the lowest conditions of earth. Thus necessity inheres as an element in freedom, but it is taken up and transmuted in freedom. Therefore man may advance through the school of necessity toward freedom. There is always the institution and recognition of law in the realization of freedom in the nation. Thus instead of forming an adverse element in the freedom of the will, necessity is involved and transmuted in it. There is in freedom the negation and transportation of necessity. But one is not therefore to identify the presence of necessity, the current of physical forces, with freedom or the will in the realization of personality.[1]

There is in man the recognition of the limitations of nature. But in recognizing this limit, and in defining it as limit, he has himself over-

Ueberweg finds an intimation of this doctrine which has had so wide an application in recent philosophy, and so wide an illustration in recent science, in the school of Pythagoras.

[1] In Mr. Martineau's argument the conception of the will in man as a person is inserted into, and carried by transfer over to the physical process. This would identify the will with mere force, and force acting in and through necessity. It is true that necessity is an element in the freedom of the will, and the education of the will at its first schooling is through necessity in the course of human life. But the physical process is not in its courses of necessity in identity with the will in personality. The conception of the will derived from the process of the physical world in itself is not even so high as that of fate.

passed it. But this implies an ideal element in the mind of man.[1]

We pass from the physical process of the world to the historical process of the world. The physical process of the world is taken up and transmuted in the historical process of the world.

There is an argument for the being of God derived from the historical process of the world. This carries thought on to the conscious life of man, and the realization of an ethical idea and freedom.

There is in this ethical order the organization and institution of the family and the nation. The family is not simply the product of physical conditions, to sustain no other relations and to subserve no other end ; and the nation is not merely the method of physical life, and to have its end in physical growth and bulk. Thus Hegel says, " the bond of the family is in love ; " and Aristotle says, " the end of the state is not simply to live, but to live nobly."

This process of the historical world which, in the realization of an ethical life, tends towards righteousness and freedom, must proceed from a force in which subsist qualities of righteousness and freedom. But these are the qualities of the will.

---

[1] " No one is aware that anything is a limit or defect until at the same time he is above and beyond it." (Hegel, *Encyklopadie*, vol. i. p. 121.)

They are the very elements of personality. The energy working in righteousness and towards freedom cannot be an indeterminate force as a thing, and cannot be determined by contingency, as a thing in relation with a thing.[1]

Thus it may be said that there is a revelation in history of the truth, or that the foundation of human society is in the truth. But truth is to be apprehended here not as the result of external observation, and not as a series of abstract propositions to be applied to the course and conditions of human life.

This is not simply the construction and application of an abstract idea, but the idea is realized in and through the determination of the moral order of the world. It is realized in the sphere of freedom; and in freedom there is the self-determination which is the integral element of personality.

[1] A recent writer finds, as the result of his research, "something in us not ourselves that works for righteousness." It is here and now; it is in us; it is not ourselves; it works for righteousness. This tendency, it is said, is not aimless; it works for righteousness and presumptively against unrighteousness. But this is the determination of a will, and of a will working in freedom, — that is, in a moral determination.

The writer implies only an empty notion of something with its drift or working. But the inference is not of an indefinite something, and it is not in things to work for righteousness. And if this be something in us "not ourselves," then man in his own personality, in the freedom of the spirit, must reject it as alien, for there can be no ground of action or of relation to it, as there would be of a person to a person.

This in one form is the evidence of the being of God; in another form it is the evidence of the presence of God through the courses of history and in the experience of the life of humanity.

CHAPTER II.

THE personalty of God is implied in the self-determination, — the perfect determination — of the being of God.

There is in personality the highest that is within the knowledge of man. It is the steepest, loftiest summit toward which we move in our attainment.

The germ and growth of grains and plants, the ebb and flow of waters, the rise and change of winds, the results of the most recent inquiry into the constitution of the suns, have not the worth and significance of personality.

In the course of human life, the relations of man as a person and with persons are deeper than his relations with that which is impersonal. That which is impersonal, in so far as it comes within the scope of our knowledge, exists in subjection to conditions of necessity, and has no power to transmute them in its process, and does not pass beyond them. It has no self-determination ; it is not determined from within, whatever be its relations to that which is without.

From that which is personal, and as the expression of its life, have come the arts and laws and literatures of the world. This appears in the highest forms of human thought, in some single phase, in the writings of Æschylus and of Shakespeare, and there the personality of Æschylus and Shakespeare is greater than their works, while their works give forms of thought which, in their elements of freedom through their ethical life and conflict, are other and higher than those which subsist in the necessary process of the physical world.

That which is personal is also construed in the institutions of society. It is involved in the life of the family and the nation. It exists in correlation with them, and through them it has its realization. There comes thence the recognition of the foundation in and through God, of the life of the family and the nation, in the historical courses of the world.

The personality of God is thus in consistence with that process of thought, through the realization of righteousness and freedom, by which there comes the manifestation of God, and from which there is derivative the knowledge of God.

The personality of God does not involve limitation. The only limitation is self-limitation, — the limit which it sets in its own self-determination.

This is its own action and for its own end, and personality in and through this is manifested.

Personality does not involve limitation. Personality has not its ground in the difference of the me and the not-me, but in the realization of the me. It has not its ground external to itself as in the limitation of the me by the not-me, but it has its ground within itself.

Personality in man exists among the limitations of the finite, but it has not its ground in these limitations. It is not prescribed and determined by physical conditions. It is not the consequent of its circumjacent condition, — and this, among finite forms, would make it only a contingency. It is not the result of certain potencies in a physical sequence; this would leave it in their operation merely a residuum. It has not its end in a determination or dissolution into the elements of the physical process.

The personality of man in its realization tends to overcome the limitations of the finite. It does this in the assertion of its own being, its own self-determination, its own freedom. It recognizes these limitations, this

"Muddy vesture of decay
That doth so grossly close us in."

It does not here and now exist beyond these limitations, but it exists in them in a life which is self-determined, and may not be determined by them.

Personality in man is impaired in the same measure in which it is determined from without. It suffers, then, the mutations which exist in the necessary process of the world, but it does not carry through them a clear and increasing purpose, and does not transmute them into freedom.

Personality with God is in substance the same as personality in man. The elements in the will, and in freedom, and in righteousness are the same.

The personality of God is infinite. There is the perfect oneness of the ideal and the real. Thought and will with him are one. In him is the absolute righteousness, the eternal truth, the infinite life.

Then to man, in the realization of his own personality, there is open the life that is infinite. The will of God is manifest that man may become one with God. God suffers the limitations of the finite that man may rise to the life that is infinite. God becomes subject to the conditions of time that man may enter into the life that is eternal.

The personality of man has its foundation in the personality of God. It could have no lower and no other ground, as there is for it the realization of the life that is infinite and eternal.[1]

[1] Lotze says: " Perfect personality is to be found only in God,

These words are the expression of a person, *Because I live, ye shall live also.*

The personality of man is not to be represented as a reflection of the personality of God. It is no remote imitation, and no faint impression of the personality of God. It is real. It has the strength of the free spirit. It moves among the fleeting forms and fading images of the finite, where shadow pursues shadow, but it is not of them. In the accident of time it is conscious of a life —

" Builded far from accident."

The personality of God is the ground of his relation with the personality of man. Without personality in God, he would, so far as the knowledge of man goes, be lower than man, and without personality in man, there would be no ground of relation to God.

.while in all finite spirits there exists only a weak imitation of personality." (*Mikrokosmus*, vol. iii. p. 576.) But personality is real : it is most real. It is not some pale outline, some dim semblance. In its advance, even, it is not, to use Shakespeare's phrase, merely "a simular of virtue." When it is said that in man there is only a weak imitation of personality, the words involve a contradiction, and in weak imitation personality is not realized but impaired.

Personality is real. It is free and enters into the freedom of God. It advances in its moral being, but this is in the life with God.

It advances through relations, but its relations are not to God as to something external; it is not simply an external relation. Lotze says truly, " the relation of a being to another being is not between them but in them." The relation, in human life, of a father and a son, which is but imperfect as the expression of the relation of the human personality to the divine personality, is yet not merely an external relation.

The personality of God is the condition of the communion of man with God. If the personality of man was only a weak resemblance, and an imperfect reflection, then also, there could be no ground of communion. There is, further, no conception of knowledge or love, which are involved in a communion, that man can attach to " a something not ourselves," or " a universum," or " an unknown," and with these terms and formulas there can be no ground for a communion. In the course of this human life, and these human relations, man is conscious of a communion which has other and higher qualities, and is not formed of physical elements, and is not subject to their conditions.[1]

The personality of God is the postulate of the knowledge of God. In this human life and these human relations, in the knowledge of a person by a person, there are elements of strength and love, elements of freedom which are deeper than those which exist in the knowledge of the physical world. The knowledge of the physical process is

---

[1] There is no ground in the physical process, for personality or for freedom. The school of Mr. Tyndall is correct within the limitations of its own thought. For in the physical process the law is that of necessity, and a person is only a sequent in the evolution of things, or a contingency in the incident of things. The distinction of a person and a thing is superfluous. For personality is then at the most only a product of physical forces, a congeries of hereditary habits and tendencies.

the result of observation and comparison; it is the fruit of research; but in human relations there are other elements. There is a knowledge which is not the result of experiment, and yet may come through experience. Thus, for instance, one will not experiment on a friend, and sympathy and love are not among the results of research. There may be in the words, *I know him in whom I have believed*, a deeper knowledge than that which man obtains through the external observation of phenomena.[1]

As the personality of man has its foundation in the personality of God, so the realization of personality brings man always nearer to God. Through the deeper knowledge of himself, through self-knowledge, man comes to the knowledge of God. As the higher realization of personality is not simply through the realization of the me and the not-me, so in the family and the nation there is a relation for man that is beyond this, it is through the me and God. Thus the institution and con-

---

[1] " For morality you must have affections, and for affections you must have beings: and atheism does not provide beings. The beings it provides are not substances and spirits. Can you love phenomena? Nature is moved indeed; and a spirit half volatile and half melancholy breathes in light, classic poetry toward all vanishing beings, even upon the sympathetic ground of a common transiency; but love by its very law tends toward a substance; it wants the solemnity of eternal being; it wants a beyond; and no being that is without this beyond can duly answer to it as an object." (Mozley, *University Sermons*, p. 47.)

tinuance of the life of the family and the nation is in God.

The personality of God is the foundation and the condition of the freedom of man. It is the source of moral strength. It is the condition of the moral responsibility of man, for this implies a relation that is other than that which exists toward phenomena or the law which is inferred from the sequences of phenomena. The self-determination of God in righteousness and freedom is the ground of the self-determination of man. It lifts man beyond the absence of nihilism, with its negations and mere transpositions, and beyond the indefinite phases of pantheism, that conception that is spatial more than spiritual, in which man loses himself, but comes not to himself. It is in contrast with the ignorance and servility that breed superstitions. The superstitious man is one who is not self-determined, and trusts in righteousness, but is determined by external and occult potencies, and yields the control of his own action to his conceit of these. The recognition of this forbids all that is abject, the degradation of reason, and the prostration of will. It overthrows all idolatries, whether before the idols of the school or the market, of the street of the city, or the assembly of the people.

It makes personality the central principle of the worlds, and, for us, the first principle of hu-

man emotion and human thought. It is the *I am
who was before all worlds;* it is one who saith *I
am that I am.* In this finite existence man exists
in conditions of necessity, but necessity is taken
up and transmuted in the self-determination of
the free spirit.

The personality of man not only has its foundation in the personality of God, but in that alone is
its eternal life. If man had no relation beyond
the physical process, if personality had no other
relations, it might not avoid the conclusion that
it was to be resolved again into the physical elements,[1] to be reproduced in other chemical poten-

---

[1] It is apart from this, that life becomes ephemeral and phenomenal.   From a recent school, Mr. Tyndall has a representation of the
personality of man, as determined within the limitations of the finite.
It is the apprehension of the life of man simply as ephemeral and
phenomenal.   Its movement is regarded as automatic and void of
real freedom.   The only hope for man is that in the mingling of the
physical elements he may impart some tint of blue to the cloud,
while the mists and exhalations of earth are mainly gray.   Shakespeare has a representation of life as phenomenal, where all personality is gone, but it is portrayed as a consequence of evil courses, it
is the issue of a life, the steps of whose advancement have been
through falsehood and murder, it is the issue of a course of awful
crime, until at last the energy of the free spirit has failed, and the
consciousness of its divine relation has gone.   In the closing scenes
of the play of Macbeth, the death of Lady Macbeth is announced,
with the comment on it.

> *Macbeth.*   Wherefore was that cry ?
> *Seyton.*   The Queen, my lord, is dead.
> *Macbeth.*   She should have died hereafter;
> There would have been a time for such a word.
> To-morrow, and to-morrow, and to-morrow,
> Creeps in this petty pace from day to day
> To the last syllable of recorded time.

cies and forms, and could have no existence apart from them. This Socrates, who drank the hemlock, might have no other hope but that he himself in the mingling of the elements might be changed into the root and liquor of that tree of hemlock. In its chemical changes it could only anticipate the shaping of the curvature of the bones of some other animal, or the imparting of some tint to the sky of some later day. This an-

*And all our yesterdays have lighted fools
The way to dusty death. Out, out, brief candle !
Life 's but a walking shadow, a poor player
That struts and frets his hour upon the stage
And then is heard no more : it is a tale
Told by an idiot, full of sound and fury,
Signifying nothing.*

But this portrayal of life as merely phenomenal, with no ground for personality and with no realization of divine and eternal relations, is given with the contrast of another life. In these closing scenes, there is the announcement of another death.

Ross. Your son, my lord, has paid a soldier's debt :
He only lived but till he was a man ; . . .
    Siward.   Then he is dead ?
Ross. Ay, and brought off the field : *your cause of sorrow
Must not be measured by his worth, for then
It hath no end.*
    Siward.   Had he his hurts before ?
Ross. Ay, on the front.
    Siward.   *Why then, God's soldier be he !* . . .
And so, his knell is knoll'd.
    Malcom.   He 's worth more sorrow,
And that I 'll spend for him.
    Siward.   He 's worth no more :
*They say he parted well, and paid his score :
And so, God be with him !*

This life is with God. This life, that is not that of fribble or of crime, is not ephemeral, it has *a worth that hath no end.*

ticipation would involve some knowledge or assumption of knowledge of another and continuous existence, which would be in suspicious contradiction to man's present brief existence. But it would be all that man would have. There would be no relation beyond the physical to justify the thought of continuous being. The personality of God is the ground of the continuous being of the personality of man.

The personality of man in its relation with men involves individuality. This individuality exists in the relations of the individual to the race, and in the development of personality through an existence subject to finite conditions. In the realization of personality as it advances in man toward the universal, this element of individuality tends to recede and disappear. But the personality of God, in his own infinite being, is not formed in the differences of a finite process, that the element of individuality should attach to it. The perfect self-determination of the self-moved one is the eternal and the infinite.

The personality of God must determine our apprehension of the attributes of God and not be determined by them. God is a person: the chiefest attribute of God is freedom, he is the self-determined one, his determination is the perfect manifestation of himself, this is the significance of the Will of God: the holiness of God is the central principle in that Will, the principle in which he cannot become other than himself: the righteousness of God is the assertion of that Will on the earth; the love of God is the expression of a person toward those who are persons.

There is a certain representation of these attributes, in which the ground assumed for them is an abstract system, a mere formalism of thought. They are subjected to formal distinctions as positive and negative, or absolute and relative, or natural and moral. These terms have no substantial ground. They indicate a mere collection of qualities which are detached and divided as the elements of some component power. They bring before us a mere accumulation of powers and then leave us to consider the attachment of these to the personality of God.[1]

The attributes of God which are thus predicated of him proceed from no inner unity as in personality. They are collected and held as something external, and then applied to him. They are

---

[1] S. Augustine says, *Quidquid de Deo dicitur, non qualitas est sed essentia.* This is true, but it is ignored in the common representations of the attributes of God, and these are enumerated not merely in their attribution to him, but in their detachment as a catalogue of qualities.

" We do not worship a law however simple and fruitful it may be; we do not worship a force if it is blind, however powerful, however universal it may be; nor an ideal however pure, if it is an abstraction; we worship only a being who is living perfection, perfection under the highest forms, — thought, love." (Caro quoted by Van Oosterzee, *Dogmatik*, vol. i. p. 247.)

often conceptions derived from another source They would in some instances even involve defect, and be regarded as alien when applied to the personality of man. They may become in many ways a diversion of thought from God. They indicate notions about God and are not derivative from God. Their postulate to which they are formally appended is often the empty notion of being, as derived from the finite existences.[1]

These attributes are often described in terms

[1] " When it is said of God what he is, then the attributes or properties are enumerated. Thus God is defined by predicates, that is, special qualities, characteristics, etc.

" These predicates are not immediate properties which are essential to his nature, but through reflection they are made subsistent, and thus the definite content for them becomes as immovably fixed as is the natural content under which God was represented in the religion of nature. The natural objects in that religion, as the sun, moon, etc., exist and these characterizations of reflection are held in the same way.

" Because the Orientals have the feeling that this is not the true way to represent God, they say that he is ' the many-named,' and that his nature is not exhausted in this specification of attributes.

" The defect in this method of defining God through predicates, from which this various and unenumerated series of attributes comes, is this, — that these predicates are only special characteristics, and there are many such whose ground is the subject in itself.

" These predicates are to express the relation of God to the world. As special properties they are not correspondent to his nature, — so the other way is adopted, — to regard them as relations of God to the world. They do not thus indicate the true relation of God to himself, but to another, — that is, to the world. So they are limited and so they come into contradiction. We are conscious that God is not thus represented in a living way, when so many properties are enumerated, one after another." (Hegel, *Philosophie der Religion*, vol. ii. p. 230.)

correspondent to some abstract argument for the existence of God. Thus the argument constructed from the physical order of the world determines the reference to him primarily of force. This conception assumes that which exists in the physical world in a certain degree and through certain correlations, and ascribes it to him in its completeness.

The conception of God which we derive from the physical process of the world and the attributes we attach to him from his relation to nature, will not be very far beyond the deification of the powers of nature. It may indicate an advance, but a very slight advance, in our knowledge of God. It may bring to us the knowledge of an energy, a first principle of force or might, — and this is always an element in personality, — and this knowledge may come to man in the beginnings of time, but it is not then that this is known as the energy of the eternal love and life. It may lead the steps of man through the cloud and whirlwind and tempest; but when their tumult is stayed there may be the recognition of a diviner voice in the conscience and the consciousness of men.

The attributes of necessity are relatively lower which are suggested through the physical process of the world. They have not the attraction which belongs to the life of the spirit, in freedom and personality. This omnipresence indicates only a force wide as the expanse of the unmeasured air. This omnipotence in the same relation indicates power which excites dread as something to be averted, except in the measure in which it is brought within the knowledge of man.

There is the source of awe and terror in physical powers, and ،the physical life of men in the course of necessity is frail and brief. But there are no powers adequate to those of personality, no elements of freedom, no traces of sympathy or love. Nature, in the stillness of the forest, with indifference to man, weaves the web of the leaf and the flower. The storm will not wait for his journey, nor the night delay for his toil.[1]

There is thus always attached to these attributes, which are the inference of the identification of God with the physical process of nature, a certain characteristic, a trace of indifference or passivity. There is power, as there is in nature, but a repose that in relation to man is constant and passionless. But the personality of God, the self-moved, the self-determined one, while it implies the highest energy, does not allow apathy.

---

[1] It is true that "we are by nature the children of impulse:" but this is not a complete representation. This power of nature working in man, and this indifference of nature to man, have their expression in that awful tragedy, — the most solemn and lofty tragedy of our literature, — King Lear. It is this power by nature working in man that becomes the subject of the drama. Thus the courtier says of the course of King Lear, "it was the bias of nature;" and thus Edmund, with his hereditary fault, is led to say, at the close, "I thought to do some good, despite my nature."

The natural attributes of God, as derived from the expression assumed for the course of physical nature, must only indicate a passionless repose, — for instance, the type in art of the face of Brahma.

The attributes of God, when wrested from personality, nor centered in its unity, are constructed after the notion of some abstract system of ethics. This scheme is set forth with certain definitions, and the attributes of God are defined in consonance with it. Thus an abstract and empty conception of sovereignty which has no ethical content is assumed; but this, in the self-determination and freedom of the will, even in a human relation, would be a defect. It is a barren conception, and is annulled in the realization of righteousness and freedom on the earth.[1] Thus in another way the attributes of justice, of relative and distributive justice, are primarily ascribed to God, while truth and love and mercy, in conformance with this scheme, are placed in a secondary grade, and are regarded in a special and reserved way. Thus a scheme of divinity is held in the place of a person.

The attributes of God are not relative, as the

---

[1] " The story of the prophets and the kings of the Old Testament is applicable to the modern world, because it is a continual witness for a God of righteousness, not only against idolatry, but against that notion of a mere sovereign Baal or Bel, which underlies all idolatry, all tyranny, all immorality." (Maurice, *Prophets and Kings*, p. 9.)

term might imply; they are essential. They are not relative, as if they were involved in certain relations, and subsisted only in these relations. They are not contingent to the world.

The attributes are not, then, the expression of certain notions in which the being of God is construed. They are not the reflective phases of human thought. They are not elements which conform to the changes of human desire; they are not measured in the varying conflict of human emotion.[1]

But in this recognition of the attributes of God the freedom, the righteousness, the goodness, which belong to God, while in him they are absolute, are in their nature the same as those existent in the personality of man. If they were not, then the goodness which appears in the life of man would be illusive, and we would be left in a world of forms, — a phantasmal world, in which the ethical is not real, and is itself void of sincerity. Then one in sincerity must come to hate it.

The perfect manifestation of God to man is in a person; it is through personality. It is only in freedom that we know the infinite, and that humanity realizes its divine and eternal relations. It is only in the fulfillment of the life of humanity

---

[1] " They are not simply the product of our intellect in reflecting on God, but have existed in essential objectivity in God, and will exist, though the activity of the distinguishing human intellect exist not." (Rothe, *Dogmatik*, vol. i. p. 45.)

in God that there is the perfect satisfaction of the spirit.

In the realization of personality in freedom man rises above the limitations of the finite, and in this, and this alone, man is brought into relations with the infinite.

Thus, as man, in the realization of personality, rises through and above the finite, it is into relations with the personality of God. It is in this that he enters into the life that is immortal. That which is open to him is the life of God.

We can rightly apprehend God, not when we consider his attributes in relation to the finite ; and thus to consider his omnipresence, his omnipotence, his omniscience, involves trivial confusions and superficial perplexities, because the ground is itself the finite, and subject to transient conditions. We can only rightly apprehend him in the life of the spirit ; we can only truly contemplate him *sub specie eternitatis ;* we can only really know his attributes of being in his own infinity and his own eternity.

CHAPTER III.

RELIGION has been defined as the disposition and conduct of man, impelled by motives of hope and fear toward a power conceived as above man; or as the active and passive relations of the finite consciousness toward an unknown; or as the recognition of the relation of man to the invisible.[1]

[1] There are certain definitions of religion to be noticed. These definitions are often the representation of abstractions. They are inconsistent with the facts in the history of religion and the facts which the writer brings in with them. They often identify the religious with the ethical, which they are necessarily led to do by their assumption that the Christ was the founder of a religion.

Their defect is thus in this assumption, — that the Christ was the founder of a religion. Then they proceed to contrive a definition that will correspond with their notion or system of this religion, and also be in some way consistent with the facts in the history of religion.

Van Oosterzee says, "Religion is the life of man in communion with God." In the preceding sentence he has said: " We discern in the most savage fetish worshiper, an inward compulsion to rise not merely above themselves and this visible world, but to the Divine." But the worshiper of the fetish is not then, as the definition implies, in communion with God. So again he says: " Religion is as old and widespread as mankind upon the earth." (*Dogmatik*, vol. i. p. 76.) But this again subverts the definition it is to expound.

" Religion is an acknowledgment of our duties toward the law of God."

The inquiry as to the development of the religious consciousness, and the induction from the

" Religion is the recognition of all our duties as if they were divine commandments." (Kant, *Religion innerhalb der Grenzen der blossen Vernunft*, iv. 1.) This identifies religion with ethics. But the actual condition of religion is often void of every principle of ethics, and an advance in an ethical life is in conflict with it. The Christian development has to contend with it, as in the religion of the Aztecs and the Hindus.

" Morality and religion are absolutely one; both are a grasping of the supersensuous. What claims to be morality without religion may indeed lead to an outwardly decorous mode of life." (Fichte, *Werke*, vol. v. p. 210.)

" Religion is the living power of morality, a power which has become conscious of its origin, and which manifests itself ceaselessly in moral achievement."

" Religion is conscious morality, a morality which, in virtue of that consciousness, is mindful of its origin from God." (J. H. Fichte, *Ethik*, vol. i. p. 23.)

"The first meaning of religion is consciousness, the highest unity between what we know and what we do, which makes it impossible that what we do should contradict what we know; as the tendency of the spirit to be one with its centre — God, is morality." (Schelling, *Werke*, vol. i. p. 55.)

These definitions are admirable; they represent a lofty conception, but they are not an inference from the facts in the history of religion, nor can they consist with those facts, nor are they admitted for one instant by the most recent expositors of religion.

But these representations, assuming that the Christ is the founder of a religion, and that it is the highest or exclusive type of religion, are compelled to adopt a definition that identifies it with an ethical life, — the ethic of the spirit.

" Religion is an active and passive relation of the finite consciousness to the creator, preserver, and ruler of the world." (Nitzch, quoted by Hagenbach, *History of Dogma*, vol. ii. p. 462). This definition has a higher justification in history.

If a definition is to be devised in indifference to the facts in the religious development of the race, simply as an abstract proposition to consist with certain abstract theories or notions, then the theories facts in the history of the religious life and condition of the race, have a higher value than any formal definition. The systems which have for their postulates definitions, and proceed with indifference to the facts, only minding the definitions, are of little service except as an intellectual exercise. They are merely the building of abstractions.

Religion is conterminous with the historical life of man. It has a history. This may be traced in monuments, customs, ceremonies, laws, arts, literatures, — the records of the race.

It is modified by the soil, the climate, and the incident of physical condition. These influences may sometimes be traced as its characteristic. They not only shape its expression, for this always partakes of the external, and in all historical forms of life must be modified by external conditions, but its very character is often moulded by physical circumstances, as conditions of soil and climate, so that it seems a product of them.

In the religious life of a race there have been often the widest contrasts. Religion has some-

may have some intellectual attraction, but it matters little what the definition is.

The defect in the last definition is that it excludes pantheistic religions, — and a large part of the religions of the world are of this character, — religions which overpass the finite, only to attain to the indefinite, not the infinite.

It is also a defect in this definition that it gives an imperfect particular, and it should add, for instance, the maker, preserver, and destroyer, — since perhaps no religion prevails more widely.

times appeared as a thing of good, and again of evil. It reflects the highest, and again the lowest impulses in the nature of man, and obtains from them its object. It has given the motive to some of the noblest, and again to some of the darkest pages of history. It is more often the expression of emotion than of the mere understanding, with which in the conduct of life, though sometimes in nobler and better ways, it is frequently at variance. It is sometimes allied with the most degrading superstitions, as in the worship of some fetish, and its services are confused with the lust and violence of men. It is sometimes the worship of animal forms or physical forces, as a river, the sun, the moon. This has frequent illustration, for instance, in the rites of the tribes of Africa, or of the Indians of the Pacific coasts, or in not a low period of civilization, in the Bacchic rites of the Greeks.

Religion has been the ally of rapine, the defense of crime, the cry of war. It has brought to its aid the fiercest persecutions. It has swept many ages and lands with its desolation, until it has come to verify the line of the Roman poet, —

"Tantum religio potuit suadere malorum."

It is often the weakness of man, who is overcome with dread before the forces of nature. It is often the investure of some external object with arbitrary qualities of will and cruel and relentless qualities of character, an object of which men are afraid, and they seek to purchase its favor or avert its wrath. Thus, the religion of a people may become not simply an index of its condition, of its cruelty and violence, but the services of religion itself may become cruel with unrestrained emotion and dark with the gloom of a disturbed imagination.

It is, again, allied with larger and nobler forms of life. It has ideals which find but an imperfect expression in nature, and it embodies its thought in the loftier types of art. It sometimes becomes in so high a degree ethical in its portrayal of human life, that it is wrought in literature in its most perfect forms, so that it furnishes the illustration of the ethical conflict of man. This is the characteristic of the great dramas and epics — the " Prometheus " and " Agamemnon " of Æschylus, the "Odyssey" of Homer, the "Æneid" of Vergil.

It is often the expression of a larger ethical conception in the historical development of a people. This has its illustration in the religion of the Romans in the early periods of their history. When in the foundation of their institutions there was the recognition of the unity and order of the family and the state, and the assertion of the authority and majesty of law, — to these religion brought its consecration, and it invested them with that solemnity which always gave dignity to the spirit of Rome.

In different countries and ages, religion is so involved in the conditions of human life, that no one taking from philosophy the canon of truth can draw the lines, and describe this as a true religion and that as a false religion. In each there are certain elements of truth, however imperfectly apprehended or rudely represented, and in each there are certain principles which indicate necessities of human nature, however imperfectly supplied.[1]

And when religion is judged by an æsthetic canon, it cannot be apprehended as altogether beautiful. It may often embody its conceptions in some monstrous or fantastic forms, some grotesque image with cruel faces and many hands, to strike terror in the minds of men. It finds the symbols of its worship in that which is lowest. It identifies man most closely with animal forms of life. It draws its attributes from the physical process, the types of its productive or destructive energies, attributes of cruelty or caprice, of irony or indifference for the condition of man. These images are often invested with some mythical or

---

[1] Schleiermacher, who in this is widely followed by recent writers, says : " Religion is constituted in feeling — the absolute feeling of dependence on God." (*Werke*, vol. iii. p. 70.) But it is not simply constituted in feeling, and while a feeling of dependence is in a certain way a right feeling and condition, it is very far from the whole or the highest condition, though it is taken up as an element in the highest. It is at most the attitude of a servant, and a deeper feeling, as well as a larger human relation, is evoked in the words, *I call you not servants but sons, I call you not disciples but friends.*

traditional significance which is a subject of interior knowledge. They may thus furnish to those who hold them in their intellectual reserve, suggestions of a certain beauty and truth. They come to be celebrated in temples of great splendor of architecture. This has often appeared with the advance of a people in its art and culture of life.[1]

But, again, religion takes on forms at variance with that which is true and beautiful. It appears in the abject degradation of one who worships the stone on which his foot has tripped, or the snake whose fang he dreads. It is seen in the tread

---

[1] The derivation of the word religion, whether that given by Cicero, or by Lactantius, or, still better, with the remote suggestion of S. Augustine, is of slight significance. And the distinction which Lactantius draws between *religio* and *sapientia*, or that of S. Augustine between *religio* and *pietas* has not, although of interest, the deepest significance.

" Religion is a disease, though a noble disease." This remarkable saying of Heraclitus, in the sixth century B. C., has been placed among the *spuria*, but, as Muller says, it has the full, massive, noble ring of Heraclitus. It is too great to be of a doubtful origin, while so remote in its source. " Heraclitus blames those who follow singers and whose teacher is the crowd; who pray to idols as if they were to gossip with the walls of houses, not knowing what gods and heroes really are. But Heraclitus nowhere denies the existence of God, or of the one Divine. Only when he saw people believing in what the singers told them about Zeus and Hera, about Hermes and Aphrodite, he seems to have marveled; and the only explanation which he could find of so strange a phenomenon was that it arose from an affection of the mind, which he physician might try to heal whenever it showed itself, but which he could never hope to stamp out altogether." (Muller, *Origin of Religions*, p. 5.)

with measured motion of the dervish, and in the squalor, the lacerated form and rigid feature of the ascetic of the Hindus. It is in its methods often wild and turbulent; it is subversive of human energy; it is destructive of institutions of order and law; it is regardless of truth and sobriety; it is alien to human freedom; it guards its domain as its own possession against the advance of thought; it is in alliance with ignorance against the beneficent influences of science; it is in conflict with elements of progress, and confronts them with its own inquisition; it thwarts natural affection, and leads the mother to abandon her offspring before some image of its devotion. Still, in nearly every town it leaves the record, it may be, of some poor child whose imagination has been tortured, or of some poor woman who has been taxed by its devices, and is left deranged and confused in mind and life by the modern revivalist.[1]

---

[1] " Religion builds by turns, and fires the world, — in its pureness the ornament and strength of society, in its perversion the scandal and scourge of nations. It supplied the first rudiments of society; it forecasts the social destination of man; — leader in all progress; vanguard of all stability; source of revolutions the most prevailing; champion of the boldest adventures; pioneer more eager than commerce; explorer more patient than science. Religion is acknowledged the mistress of arts. She reared the temples that make Egypt venerable, and the marbles that made Greece renowned. While gratefully acknowledging the multifold service of the great benefactress, we cannot forget the mischief and the woes that have often accompanied these gifts and goods. We cannot forget that religion has been a worker of evil. No agent that has wrought in earthly scenes has been more prolific of ruin and wrong. The wildest aber-

In its more prevalent and in its recent forms, it recognizes in the object of its fear and devotion alike the preserver and the destroyer, whether it be the Vishnu and Siva of the Hindu, or the Apollo of a later culture, who is "healer and slayer of men." It is, in some ways, averse to a high ideal; the picture which is rude in outline and dim in color is preferred to that which has greater excellence. The Apollo, with its beautiful disdain and its lines of light and strength, is remanded to a museum; while the dark image of a Jupiter, formed in some later and lower school of art better serves its uses, and is made to stand as the image of a High Pontiff, and its foot is worn with the kisses of the faithful.

In the comparative history of religions, the development of the religious spirit may be traced more perfectly, perhaps, in India. From India have come religions which have been sustained by a larger number, and have survived greater crises, and have prevailed through more extensive territories. No other people has been so deeply religious. When the vast multitude, the long centuries, the extended territories are considered, no other history is so impressive and so pathetic. In no other people have there been forms, traditions, days,

rations of human nature, crimes the most portentous, the most devastating wars, persecutions, hatred, wrath, and bloodshed, more than have flowed from all sources beside, have been its fruits." (Hedge, *Ways of the Spirit* p. 36.)

discipline of life, so carefully observed or so completely interpenetrated with their religion. Nowhere else have there been built so many shrines, so spacious temples; nowhere else have there been penances so long, pilgrimages so frequent, fasts and trials so severe and unrelenting. Its service is so costly, its gifts so many, its devotions so constant, its asceticism so patient.[1]

Religion, in its higher forms, everywhere may express the sorrow and pain of the human spirit— in the limitations of the finite ; in the darkness of its ignorance, so shadowed by the uncertainty of its brief years; in the struggle of its own mortality; in the depth of its degradation, of which there may come an increasing conviction ; in the

---

[1] " Comparative religion shows that Christianity is one among many forms." " It can only be understood when taken as one step in the religious history of mankind." " Idolatry is one form of religion." (Parker. See Weiss, *Life of Parker*, vol. ii. p. 56.) In a work indicative of common thought, the writer says: " Notwithstanding their many differences of opinion, all Christians agreed in believing that, of all historical forms of religion, Christianity was most worthy of God, and best adapted to the religious wants, etc." (Hagenbach, *History*, vol. ii. p. 463.) In consistence with this, that, which describes the Christian revelation as a religion, would make all Christian men agree that it was relative, and might be at some date displaced by some form of religion yet more worthy and of better adaptation. The confusion arises from assuming that it is a form of religion among the religions of the world.

On the relation of the religions of the world see Maurice, *The Religions of the World;* Hegel, *Philosophie der Religion*. The latter is mainly a study in the comparative history of religions. The writings of Mr. Conway and Mr. Frothingham are also of interest on this subject.

4

conflict with evil forces which it yet knows are alien to itself: and through all these it may express its unselfish aims, its lofty aspirations, its unconquerable hopes. It may be stirred with that which is better, and with the images of that which is enduring, and is not subject to decay, nor transient in the transience of the world.

In its higher forms the religious mind becomes the evidence of the greatness of man, which has no finite measures. It becomes pervaded with the awe and humility, the reverence and adoration, which are the expression still of the exaltation of man. It becomes filled with images drawn from the deep life of the world. Religion is then the ally of poetry and art in their nobler forms. It brings before the mind images of holy beauty, with no stain of decay. It transfigures the sorrow of earth. It is indifferent to the finite, and is itself the morning and evening of the spirit. It breathes the air of the happy isles; it sails into the sunset beyond the far Cathay. It is led by a mystic devotion; it is lost in the rapture of its joy. It bows at the shrines which it has built with the heart's adoration.

It rears temples which are the rest of the sorrow and the loneliness of earth; where weakness may pray and penitence may weep; where anguish may seek to quench its tears; where grief may strive to forget its pain, and hope to reillumine its gloom. In its weariness of the restless play of human passion, it seeks the obliteration of the finite, and turns to some abode of calm and passionless repose. It recognizes the pathos of the closing day, the changing seasons, the autumn with its falling leaves, the swift advance of age, the loneliness of the grave.

The forces which may modify and restrain the course of the religious mind are traced through the whole circumstance of life. They are, for instance, the obligations of domestic and civil relations, the subjection to necessity in the requisition of the labor of the day, and the economy of life that encourages a sober realism. Man has to look to other forces, to the life of nature in its more healthful influences, to society, to literature, to poetry, to art, for restraints which may control the ignorance, the emotional excess, and the imaginative gloom of the religious mind.[1]

Philosophy, also, has only a scant representation in formal definitions. To assume the statement of the boundaries of a country as the actual description of it is better than the limitations of a formal definition.

Philosophy, in its larger outline, has been defined as the course of thought which has its spring

---

[1] Hegel says, with consummate beauty and depth of expression, "In morality, the harmony of religion with actuality, with the world as it is, is brought to existence and perfection." (Hegel, *Philosophische Abhandlungen*, p. 400.)

in man with the love of knowledge; or the reflection of thought on the process of being; or the
attainment toward truth by the way of reason.
The larger apprehension of philosophy than any
definition, may be derived from its history; but it
is not to be forgotten that, while there is a history of philosophy, there may be in a deeper sense
a philosophy of history. Philosophy apprehends
an empiric process in history, but passes beyond it
to that which is metempirical.

Religion and philosophy, although there has
been a difference in their comparative process,
and although they have often been in conflict,
have an immediate relation. They have for their
object the same goal. In each the end is the
absolute, the attainment and realization of the
truth; in each the end is God, the goal of the
aspiration and endeavor of the spirit. Each in its
advance conforms with an ethical principle, — in
humility. The process of the one is in thought,
of the other in worship; the one moves through
reflection, the other through emotion; but each,
in its development, involves the other, as it has
for its aim the truth.

Hegel, in one of his letters, says, "Philosophy
seeks to apprehend by means of thought the
same truth which the religious mind has by faith."
He repeats this: "The object in philosophy is
upon the whole, the same as in religion. In both

the object is truth in that supreme sense in which God, and God only, is truth."[1] Religion and philosophy in their end are one.

But while religion and philosophy thus often move in parallel lines and toward the same end, in certain respects, it is necessary to place philosophy above religion. This is involved in its very method. There is an element of thought which formulates religion, and opens a critical inquiry as to its contents. It proceeds through a dialectic of reason. There is thus a philosophy of religion.[2]

Philosophy has often given a profounder expression to the ethical conflict of man than it has found in religion, while, in their higher forms, they are so closely blended. Philosophy has advanced through the most profound experience of the relation of man to the truth, that is, the reality of things. It has not been a formal process, a barren speculation, as the blank of light, and void of all

---

[1] Hegel, *Vermischte Schriften*, vol. ii. p. 520.

It may be said that man is by nature a religious animal, in the same way that it may be said that he is philosophical; or that he has a philosophical or religious nature. The nature of the religious, the philosophic, the scientific mind is an interesting subject. These are all in their relative service determined by a strictly ethical measure.

[2] "It has been said that religion is at the cradle of every nation, and philosophy at its grave." (Morley's *Rousseau*, vol. ii. p. 259.) This has a certain truth, and religion appears more often as a constructive force in society, while philosophy is of later culture and reflective.

content, but it has wrought as truly as religion
with things of life. There has been through it
the expression of that which is deepest in the life
of man.

The progress of philosophy also has often been
indicative of a higher historical development in a
people. It has given a firmer maintenance to the
authority of law, to the unity and order of states.
It has furnished no less impressive sanctions to
the domestic and civil and political relations of
men, in the family and the commonwealth and
the nation. Its work toward the same end with
religion, has been pursued with a no less enduring
patience and a constant devotion. It has been
animated by an enthusiasm that could be sustained only by the noblest ends. It has been followed with a disregard of merely selfish interests
and an indifference to worldly aims. Its course
has been characterized by a humility and reverence as real as that which has prevailed in religion. There has sometimes been a collision between them, and this has assumed a tragic form.
Socrates was condemned to die as an enemy to
the religion of the state. The accusation against
him was that he was an enemy to the common religion of the times in which he lived. The world
will continue to read the story of the untimely
death of the martyr of philosophy, wrought by
Plato into the very argument of immortality, and
will hold it among its imperishable possessions.

Philosophy has often been connected with a higher ethic, and furnished the aid toward a higher ethical life, than religion. If its influence in this respect has not in any one period prevailed so widely, it has been more enduring and survived greater crises. The Ethics and the Political Ethics of Aristotle and Plato have had a continuous influence upon the actual life of the race. They have been translated into languages then unspoken, and have shaped the thoughts of a thousand tribes with their advance toward a historic life in lands which were then uninhabited. The cultus and system of the religions that were contemporary with them have utterly perished; there comes to them no revival. But these works still have power in the lives of men. They have, it is true, this advantage in the close relation of philosophy with literature, that the greatest masters in philosophy have also been the greatest masters in literature.[1]

[1] If it was ever given to any one man to express the prophetic hopes and longings of the human soul, to give voice to

— "the prophetic soul of the wide world,
Dreaming on things to come,"

it was given to Plato. There has been in no religion so full an expression of the hopes and desires of men which prefigure the revelation of God. The common thought is given by Van Oosterzee: "It is certain that Plato has more distinctly than any one else expressed the want which has been supplied by the revelation ot the light of the world." (*Dogmatik*, vol. i. p. 113.) The work of Aristotle also has brought the most profound justification to the Christian theology. This was recognized in the greater ages of the theology of the church.

Religion and philosophy both have their fulfillment in the revelation of God in the Christ. The long conflict and the travail through suffering and sacrifice of religion, and the toil through doubt and denial, the sincerity of conviction, the wrestle of thought for the truth, of philosophy; — the effort of religion and philosophy, have their fulfillment in the revelation of God.

They have been formed in the slow and arduous ascent of man. They appear through the dissolution and resolution in the reflective movement of thought and emotion, of the relations of man with the finite and the infinite. They bear the impress of many tribes and many lands, through the ages of the world. It may be given to faith, it may be the ascertainment of reflection, that no step through this evolution of society has been inconsequent, and no effort vain.

Religion and philosophy have both exerted a determinate influence on the development of the Christian faith and doctrine. The hope and aspiration of religion, the desire of the nations, has found its end in the Christian revelation. But this influence has been more potent through philosophy. Thus, in the speculation of Plato and of Aristotle, the Christian doctrine has found its justification, and their influence has determined the course and development of great schools of Christian thought.

The Revelation of and in the Christ is not a religion, and it is not a philosophy.

It cannot be brought within the scope or province of any definition of religion that has a justification in history. It is not the product of any distinctive religious progress; and, further, it has not its origin in any system of speculation, nor in the reflective order of thought. It is not a philosophy, but its relation to philosophy is as clear and distinct as to religion.

It is not within the process of the history of religions. It is not to be brought as one stage into the development, or as one subject in the comparative study of religions. It is not related to them as one individual form to another, nor as the universal to the individual; for when they are embraced as a whole, it is other and more than they. It can no more take the place to which it is invited among the various religions of the world than the figure of the Christ can take its place in the Pantheon of a Julian.

If it be assumed that it is strictly a religion, it is not clear in its relation to philosophy. For philosophy will still maintain its claim to hold it in subjection to its canons, to determine its position in relation to the continuous progress of speculative thought, and will still seek for a real and substantial truth.

The Christ does not come into the world as the

founder of a religion, and this revelation is not
set forth as an institute or a system or a cultus of
religion.

The Old Testament is not primarily the record
of a religion, or of a system or science of religion.
It is not the revelation of a religion,[1] but it is the
revelation of God to the world; his revelation to
the family which he has formed, and to the nation
which he has founded, and thence to the world.

The ritual which it contains is subordinate in
this historical, this domestic and political development. There may be traces, in the forms and
services, which the scholar may discern, of the influence of the religions of Egypt and Babylon, and
the countries of the Tigris and Euphrates valleys,
but it is primarily a revelation which is other than
these. It is throughout in conflict with these religions, through its revelation of God, as One and
invisible, who will put away all the idolatries of
men, and will establish his righteousness on the
earth.

It is a record of the unity and order of the
family and the nation, as these endure, in the organic life of humanity.

---

[1] " In other books you have the records of a *religion*. You are
told how a people introduced this worship and that ceremony; how
their soothsayers told them of services that they had neglected; how
their priests enforced new propitiations. Here you have nothing of
the kind. All the religion which the priests or the people introduced
— the worship on hills and in groves, the calves, the altars to Baal
— is noticed to be denounced; a righteous king proves his righteousness by sweeping it away." (Maurice, *Sermons*, vol. iii. p. 507.)

It averts the attention from a further world, without affirmation and without denial in regard to it, and is intent upon the eternal and infinite presence dwelling in the here and now. Thus it is an even question with a scholar whether it recognizes a world on and beyond and the immortality of the soul, in the common use of this term. Thus it differs from the subjects which form the staple of the religious books of the world.

The Commandments, which are given at an early age, and are continuous and formative with the people, have no distinctive religious quality; they are formed in and become themselves the maintenance of institutions of domestic and civil and political order.

It is throughout the revelation of one God, who is invisible, of whom there can be no graven image made by the hands of men, whose name is the Almighty, the I Am, the Eternal, who is with the family and with the nation in the attainment of their life in the life of humanity. It was in this and in the acknowledgment of the Commandments as the ground of freedom, and in the consequent transition from slavery to freedom, and in the actualization of righteousness, that there were the sources of conflict with the religions which the people sought constantly to introduce. This ethical course is brought out with the strongest contrasts. It is the burden of the prophets borne through all the ages of their history. When the king says he has reserved the best of the sheep and oxen to sacrifice unto the Lord, the prophet answers, *to obey is better than sacrifice, and to hearken than the fat of rams.* The words which the prophets repeat as one long refrain through historic periods are, *the new moons and sabbaths; your new moons and your appointed feasts my soul hateth: they are a trouble unto me; I am weary to bear them; wash you, make you clean; cease to do evil, learn to do well.* The charge which is brought against the people is their taking the forms and formulas of a service instead of God. They said no longer, *where is Jehovah? but the temple of the Lord, the temple of the Lord.* To repeat the expression which Kant uses, their fault was in the substitution of the services of religion for the service of God.[1]

In the course of the development of the history of the world, in the fullness of time, the Christ does not come to man as the Founder of a religion. The institution of a religion is not the subject of the records of the New Testament. In recent times an eminent man, and of eminent influence upon his age, has announced himself as the Founder of the religion of humanity.

---

[1] " The charge which God by his prophets brings against his people in the last days is the taking his ordinances instead of himself. See Isaiah and all through Jeremiah. They said not, where is Jehovah? but the temple of the Lord, the temple of the Lord." (Erskine, *Memoirs*, p. 157.)

The writings of the New Testament, as we pass again to their content, have not a religion, nor the institution nor the revelation of a religion, for their subject. It is the revelation of the Christ in man, and the infinite and eternal life of man. In these writings the very word *religion* does not appear. There is no word which could identify their subject distinctively with a religion or a philosophy. Thus there is in the writings of S. John no reference to the subject. The Gospel and the Epistles of S. John are concerned with a revelation, and the manifestation of an eternal life.[1]

---

[1] " Thus we learn what work it is our missionaries have to do when they go into heathen lands. It may be, before they leave their own country, they think that their business is to rouse the natives of those lands to what they would call a sense of religion, an interest about their souls, a conviction of the shortness of life, the anticipation of an approaching judgment and eternity. They can scarcely stir a step in any of these countries without discovering traces of a sense of religion, of an interest about the soul, of an anticipation of death, of a dread of what is to follow death, to which they were quite unused on their own soil. If they have no other vocation than this, if they have not learnt that this is not even a part of the message which they are to carry with them, they may soon regret that they ever crossed the seas. They will find that the task which they came to perform has been done and is doing more effectually by the Yogis and Fakirs, whose influence they wish to destroy. Unless they come with a gospel concerning God; unless that gospel enables them to meet the anxieties about religion, about the soul, about death, about the future, which lie like a dead weight upon the faculties and energies of tribes which have proved themselves capable, and are still capable, of noble thoughts and great deeds; unless they can turn the thoughts of immortality and judgment into moral and quickening thoughts, they are not going out upon the errand on which S. Paul and the missionaries of his day went; they are not

In the writings of S. Paul the rare use of a corresponding word is very significant. It finds no place except in infrequent and indirect reference. S. Paul lived among sects and societies, into which the nation was divided, that were of an exclusive and intensive religious character. He describes his early life, — his life before his conversion, and before the revelation of the Christ and its light was given to him : *after the most straitest sect of our religion, I lived a Pharisee.* The Greek word which he uses is not of very noble lineage nor character, nor of the larger significance of the English word — religion. S. Paul, in a phrase of critical significance, says to the Athenians, as he stands in sight of their altars and temples, where their services and processions are so frequent and imposing, *I perceive that in all things ye are too religious.* The characteristic words which S. Paul uses are of a revelation in the Christ and the righteousness of the Spirit. S. James has a phrase in which the word is assumed in the common translation, which may be noticed for its ethical significance, " pure and undefiled religion is to visit the widow and the fatherless." This would obviously be deficient by its limitation of religion to the ministry of charity. The word should be translated ritual. It is not of grave importance

carrying the news of a redemption, they are not testifying of that glory which was manifested in the Person of Jesus Christ to the world." (Maurice, *Sermons,* vol. i. p. 126.)

to the subject, but it has thus an illustrative and beautiful significance. The true ritual is not of form and processional, but in actual charity.

In the writings of S. Paul there is only an indirect reference to the development of religion or the speculation of philosophy. It must be admitted that nothing could be more alien to his thought than a discourse on the advantages or the excellences of religion. He is concerned neither with the experiences of religion nor the courses of philosophy. But not only the very word religion has in these writings no correspondent, but their content is other than that. It is a revelation; it is of righteousness; it is of righteousness by faith; it is of the ethic formed in the knowledge of God; it is of a judgment in the presence of the infinite and eternal, in which alone is the right judgment, by individuals and by nations, of this finite world; it is a judgment of the world, but by One who has lived on this earth, and is risen from the dead. This in one form is verified in the deepest human experience, as it has its anticipation in one of the loftiest works of philosophy, the dialogue of Plato on the immortality of the soul. The thought which is always deeper than his formal argument is that in the presence of the death of one we love we know the infinite in the life of humanity. This verifies itself to man that love is stronger than death.

The outline alone remains of the large dis-

course of S. Paul at Athens; but that discourse
was of the revelation of God, of righteousness, of
the judgment of the world by one risen from the
dead.   It was not the announcement nor the commendation of a religion to the Athenians.

In the writings of the New Testament, the
Christ uses phrases that were common in his day,
— words derived both from philosophy and religion. This appears in terms pertaining to philosophy, — as the word, truth, the eternal, freedom; and in terms pertaining to religion, — as
prayer, faith, heaven. But these words are used
very sparingly, while they are penetrated with a
new meaning, and another and higher import is
given to them. His words are mainly drawn from
the daily life of man, as the Father, the Son, the
Son of man, and again, from the contemporary
forms of political life, as the King, the Kingdom
of God.

The law of all forms, which subjects them to
the uses of humanity, and pervades them with
a principle which is wrought into the actualization of the freedom of humanity, is in the
words, *the sabbath was made for man, and not
man for the sabbath.* This is universal in its application, and from one of the earliest and most
sacred of all forms the princ'ple is derived by
which all are regarded.

In words of yet more significant import, whose
offense to the religious societies of his age could

not be exceeded, and which have the same import for the religious societies of every age, the Christ as he walks across the fields on the sabbath day says, *in this place is one greater than the temple.*

These words were used by S. Paul afterwards in the deeper imagery in which human life is portrayed in the life of the Spirit, as he writes, *know ye not that your body is the temple of the Holy Ghost?* There cannot be a further remove of the religious order than in the representation of man as the temple of the Spirit.

The Christ was a divine witness for the service of humanity. It is a divine precedent that is not superseded by any form; *therefore did the Jews persecute Jesus, and sought to slay him, because he had done these things on the sabbath day. But Jesus answered them, My Father worketh hitherto, and I work.*

It has been said that every religion consists primarily of a cultus and a doctrine. This has an entire historical justification. But this cultus and doctrine, in the words of the Christ, are transmuted into an ethical and a universal principle. Thus the law of a cultus, or worship, is given in the rubric: *not here nor at Jerusalem; they that worship the Father must worship him in spirit and in truth.* The same principle was to be repeated again, in the diversion of thought from the earthly Jerusalem, the city girt by the Syrian

5

mountains, and in the realization of that which is universal; *the Jerusalem which is above is free, which is the mother of us all.*

As it is with a cultus, so it is with a doctrine of religion; it is at once transmuted into an ethical process and realization; *he that doeth the will shall know the doctrine.* This is given conversely in words of the most profound ethical import; *ye shall know the truth, and the truth shall make you free.*

The Christ had at no time an identity, even the most remote, with any of the great sects or societies which represented and embraced the distinctive religious life of his age. He had no connection with the Scribe or the Sadducee or the Pharisee.[1] The strongest contrast was seen in the character of the Pharisee. The Pharisee was not a man of mere pretense; he was the type of a strictly religious man, but one who cared more for religion than for humanity.

The Christ, in the beginning of his work, as he went forth into the world, went to a marriage festival. He did not withdraw himself from the actual life of men. The reproach brought against him by the religious sects and societies of his age

---

[1] "The Pharisaical aspirant assumed evil as the ground from which he started. Evil was the condition of his race. Every step that raised him above evil raised him above mankind. The nearer he approached to the Being he worshiped, the further he was from those among whom that Being had placed him." (Maurice, *Sermons*, vol. ii. p. 333.)

was, *he eats with publicans and sinners ; behold the friend of publicans and sinners.*[1]

The apostles whom he called and sent forth into the world were among common men, as one who sat at the customs and one who was a fisherman.

There is in the words of the Christ the directory for no penance, nor shrine, nor pilgrimage. There is the pattern for no altar nor temple. The rites which appear in various ways in every historical religion are not recognized.

The Christ institutes no cultus of worship and prescribes no system of dogma. There is no suggestion of form of worship or formula of doctrine. The blessing which he gives is of those who act and suffer in the life of humanity. It is of the gentle, of those who mourn, of those who suffer persecution for righteousness, of those who hunger after righteousness.

The conflict and transition from the religions of men to the life of the Spirit, the realization of truth and freedom in humanity, was to be borne on through the coming ages. The Christ foretells to his disciples this conflict, not as a casualty

---

[1] " Jesus was emphatically a man of the world. The daily walks of men were familiar to his feet; their daily joys and sorrows and all their wants familiar to his heart. When he went to the marriage feast he went as a wedding guest. When he went among publicans and sinners, he sat at their tables without reserve, and shrank from no contact with the daughters of vice. Religion might flaunt her sanctimonies, he wore no phylactery. he suffered no sabbath to check his humanity, and no tradition to bind his freedom." (Hedge, *Ways of the Spirit*, p. 108.)

of their lives, but as the sequence of a principle
that was to be realized : *they shall put you out of
the synagogues ; yea, the time cometh that whosoever killeth you will think that he doeth God service.
These things will they do unto you, because they
have not known the Father nor me.*

The characteristic event which marked the crisis, the close of one age and the opening of another
age, an æonian day, was the destruction of the
temple. And it was not simply the end of one
age and the beginning of another age; it was not
simply the close of the dispensation of the law
and the beginning of the dispensation of grace ; it
was the destruction of the temple. The Christ
had gone into the temple, but it was to affirm that
which would lead, in its realization, to the overthrow of the temple. The worship henceforth
was to be that in which none had need to journey
far, nor to go on pilgrimages to distant shrines or
cities to enter the doors of the temple. As he
went out of the temple, *some spake of the temple,
how it was adorned with goodly stones. Jesus
said, Seest thou these great buildings, there shall
not be left one stone upon another, that shall not be
thrown down.* The destruction of the temple was
the sign of the coming of the Son of man ; his
own person was that temple, in which God might
meet man, and man might meet God.

This principle was to be borne on to the close.
It finds a constant illustration. In the closing

events of this age, the accusation of the Jews against the Christ was on the ground that he was an enemy of their religion. He was charged with blasphemy. But in that hour in which he was confronted with this charge, there was the expression of no vision which brought into light the symbols of the worship of this earth, no refrain borne on through recollections of anthems and litanies. There was the utterance of those words which spoke of the eternal, the glorified life of humanity in that fulfilled vision: *Hereafter shall the Son of man sit on the right hand of the power of God.*[1]

The difference between the revelation of the Christ and all religions is ultimate. But it consists with the fact that this revelation is manifested to and in humanity. It is one with the life of righteousness, the life of the spirit. Through the revelation in the Christ the religions of the world become transmuted, as in Him has been manifested that foundation of human life which they but vainly sought, and on this earth could not find. They looked through the decay of all things for that which was beyond decay and was indestructible, but it was not in thought, or emo-

[1] " In religious books we find the death of Jesus chiefly, almost exclusively pressed, whereas in the Scriptures we find that the Apostles were called to be witnesses of his resurrection. See *Acts* ch. i. v. 22; ii. 32." (Erskine, *Memoirs*, p. 116.)

tion, or desire, and in Him was revealed that life
which does not suffer decay nor yield to the corruption of the grave. It was through death to
the resurrection, the life that is here and now in
the life of the spirit, but the life that is infinite,
the life that is eternal.

This contrast is borne on to the close ; — in the
last vision, the types of that historical process,
of which S. John the Divine has written, are not
drawn from those of which the imagination, when
filled with religious conceptions of an individual
character, can have any intimation. Its types are
drawn from the most varied activities in the common life of humanity. They are of a city, but
the glory of God doth lighten it, that there be no
need of the sun or of the moon; and of that city
it is written, *I saw no temple there.* These words
consist with no order of strictly religious thought,
and have no parallel in the religions of the world.

There are certain consequences involved in the
exposition of this revelation as a distinctive religion that may be noticed.

Religion and certain religious sentiments and
notions are made the substitute for this revelation.
The phases of the religious imagination, the vague
aspirations, and the variable moods of the mind,
often its unrestrained desires when carried away
by impulse and disturbed emotion, are made the
sum and fulfillment of this revelation. That which

man in his religious effort has devised about God is made the substitute for that which God has made known of himself.[1]

There is another consequence parallel with this, which follows from the apprehension and representation of this revelation strictly as a religion. It is brought with other religions within the pursuits of an eclectic school of religions. This may be joined with an agnostic school. It writes inscriptions, but to an unknown God. It is very religious; it regards all religions as equal and the same in their origin. This, then, is apprehended strictly as one religion among these various religions. Thus it defines their relative value; it composes their anthologies; it forms a miscellany of their various precepts; it has represented the Christ as one among the founders of religions, and it finds in the course of the Christian life in history only the institution of a system of religion. This

---

[1] It has been made a criticism of the services of the Church and its offices of prayer that wide ranges of religious aspiration and emotion are left out. They have no expression. The characteristic phrases are those which speak of the manifestation and advent, the resurrection and ascension, the redemption of the world, an eternal life, and a service which is perfect freedom. There is the widest contrast between the service of the Church and that whose characteristic is the expression of religious emotion and aspiration.

There are religious sects or societies that trace their correspondence in their origin and order back to the synagogue of the Jews as it was in the time of Christ. But the correspondence which the Christ uses is of the family and of political societies and institutions as the kingdom of heaven.

school may have a value in its aid toward the study of the comparative religions of the world. But it illustrates the fact that this revelation, when it is apprehended simply as one religion among others, may become the most inconsequent and incomplete of all. It is devoid of life; it is reduced to broken fragments, mere words of counsel and exhortation to religious conduct. The school is one of clever criticism, of intellectual subtlety, of large but vague aspirations, of pale negations, of weak but irregular pietism. It may be, as S. Paul describes the agnostics at Athens, too religious.

The defect in this mode of thought appears in another form, in the assumption of a controversy between religion and righteousness, — between religion and morality. This distinction has no ground in the writings of the Old and New Testament, unless it be in the contrast of the revelation of God and his righteousness with the religions which prevailed in the world. It is not that religion and morality are there represented as in a formal identity; these phrases are set aside. If morality be regarded only as a course of external decorum, or as the economy of the individual resultant from a prudential estimate of the promiscuous advantages of life, or as a hereditament in the evolution of man through a life determined by physical necessity, then it has no consistence with this revelation, which presumes a will that acts in freedom, and the manifestation of a living God who will establish righteousness on the earth. This ethical life, the life of the righteousness of the spirit, cannot be apart from God, as there can be no true conception of conscience which does not affirm the being of God.

The terms of this distinction, however, of religion and morality, not only are alien to these writings, but, among different peoples and ages, religion is of worth mainly in the degree in which, to use Hegel's profound expression, it has been brought into identity with morality. Thus even the sacrifice it calls forth in life, in its highest act, has a value in the measure in which it is determined by a moral emotion and for a moral end. There have been far larger numbers who, from generation to generation, in the devotion and abnegation of their sacrifice, have thrown themselves before the car of Juggernaut; but the world counts beyond these the three hundred who laid down their lives in the pass at Thermopylæ, in obedience to the laws, and this gives to that field an immortal interest.

The defect in the apprehension of this revelation as a religion is apparent in the religious and philosophical systems of the preceding century. It was carried through the assumption of a distinction between a natural and revealed religion. That was a time when the message to men was the commendation of religion to an enlightened patronage. It was an age when men could build monuments alike to faith and hope and religion. It was to be followed by a school of culture, which could talk of " the state and art and religion ; " but the revelation of God cannot be brought into this catalogue.

There is a further defect in this apprehension, which is to be noticed, in the fact that religion and certain religious sentiments and notions are maintained as the substitute for this revelation. The forms of the religious imagination, the phases of religious emotion, the conceptions of the religious mind, control and determine this revelation, but they are not controlled and determined by it. These conceptions still hold their place, and are made to mould the Christian revelation instead of being moulded by it. The old heavens still are over us. Those words of deepest and divinest import were long since spoken; *The kingdom of heaven is within you ;* but not yet may we receive them in their universal and human significance ; if we accept the words it must be as a type or shadow, and allowing no reality. Thus the forms and conceptions of ancient religions determine our thought; they still prevail. They rule us from their buried urns. The gods of those imaginative forms, whether dark and cruel, or light and beautiful with the changing forms of life, have vanished, and the temples and shrines are sought no longer by men, but the religious con ceptions and images still control us; they do but slowly fade. They shape themselves in the systems of men, and still determine this revelation, and are but slowly transmuted by its spirit. This may be traced in every form and phase of religious thought.

The divine and eternal sacrifice, in the coming and life and death of the Christ on the earth, is interpreted in the preconceptions of the religions of men. The light in which it is portrayed is darkened with the awful rite, and lurid with the glare of the fires which burn on the altars of pagan sacrifice.

The inspiration of the Spirit, which is given to men in the life of the spirit, and which, therefore, has not and cannot have its postulate in the mere limitations of the finite, is held within the style of these religions. It is regarded as the inspiration of the letters and pages of the sacred books. It is no longer the utterance of the living word, but is restricted within the conception of the pagan oracle.

Thus, again, the representation of the divine judgment is that which found expression, although often in a serious and profound form, in the greater of the pagan religions and philosophies, as in the Gorgias of Plato. It is represented not as an object to be sought, and a manifestation of truth, and the realization of righteousness on the earth, but as a doom to be averted and a power

to be dispelled. The judgment, most often as portrayed in the Greek philosophies and in the Teutonic religions, is made the substitute for that
which the Christ has given, which is the realization strictly of an ethical principle and an ethical
spirit in the life of humanity.

Thus, the representations of heaven and hell
take on the imagery devised in the religions of
the world, and divested of an ethical character,
they are employed with a more potent effect.
These had an intenser expression in the Teutonic religions, with the tribes and peoples that
came from the German forests, than that which
had prevailed in the Roman or Greek religions.
Rome was practical, and had a profound sense of
law and order and their obligations. Her religion
was built on the validity of law and social obligations, and penetrated with convictions of the authority and sacredness of the family and the state,
and of the judgments which come upon a people
with the violation of their bonds. But it was,
almost as little as Judea, occupied with a nether or
an other world. It was not attracted by the images
in which its joys were portrayed, nor repelled by
its penalties; it was not allured nor alarmed by
these, while in the Greek and the Teutonic religions these took a darker form. In the Greek
there was some lightness in the pictures of the
elysian fields, while in the Teuton there was the
portrayal of a sombre, though sometimes grotesque

imagination. These are only surpassed in the awful conceptions which fill the religions of India. These still hold their place with the peoples who have inherited the Teutonic and Indian traditions. They have their reaffirmation; they give form and color to the revelation of the Christ and the life of the spirit, and it is but gradually that they are moulded and transmuted by it in the realization of the life of righteousness, the life of truth and freedom. The representations of these subjects in the higher periods of these religions and philosophies may even be nobler than some of those which still in some ages prevail. The representation of the judgment in the Greek philosophy, as in the Gorgias of Plato, and of heaven and hell in the Teutonic religion, serve as illustrations of this.

This fact has also, in the external phases of religion and religious history, a significant illustration, which may be noticed simply as an illustration of the subject. The forms and festivals of ancient religions reluctantly yield their ground. The student of history may trace the adoption from certain ages, ages of ignorance and decadence of faith, of forms and usages from different religions. These forms and festivals still impress their character upon events, and remain by transposition, as some saturnalia passes into a carnival at Rome. There are still sacred and secular days, and holy and profane things. There are shrines and pilgrimages, and the strange beauty with which the religious imagination invests the character of the shrine and the pilgrim moulds the thought, as some unfulfilled symbol in the life of man.

There may be traced in certain Christian centuries the adoption, from the east, apparently through some remote association, of patterns, forms, ceremonies, modes of dress and service; these are correspondent with those of Buddhism. There was, it may be in the fourth and again in the sixth centuries, an introduction from oriental religions, from India or Persia, of systems of penance and monasticism, and even the designs for shrines, and the colors and embroideries for robes and dresses. This, in an intellectual form, has also reappeared in some schools with the study of the literature of Buddhism and the philosophic culture of pessimism.

The graver issue of the substitution of conceptions derived from pagan religions, — as those of sacrifice and inspiration and judgment and the further worlds, for the revelation which God has made of himself in the Christ, — is that at last conceptions derived from these religions come to be attached to the conception of very God. He becomes himself a Baal, a Moloch, or a Siva; he is pacified by the suffering and death of his children; his presence is in a temple; his appearing is through the doors of a shrine; his revelation is

the sacred books; his coming again is an event of
historical circumstance in the formal process of
history. When these conceptions of pagan religions are attached to him, his character and relation to humanity are brought into correspondence
with them; or, again, he is identified with nature,
— with the nature of things, as in the religions
of nature. Thus, as his investure is with the traits
ascribed to a Moloch, or with those drawn from
the physical process of the world, this conception
is substituted for the revelation of the name of
the Father and the Son and the Holy Spirit.

But again, the substitute for this revelation is
simply the expression of religious sentiments. Instead of the revelation of God to man we have
the sentiments and feelings of man about God.
This is a school of poetry and music in its shorter
and weaker forms.; it furnishes the productions of
a religious sentimentalism; it sets aside the divine
commandments which are the ground of social
order; it identifies the character of God with the
physical process of the world. This becomes in
another form the worship of nature; it regards
the prodigality of nature, and makes this its principle, as another school has made the severity of
nature its principle, and prodigality and severity,
profusion and destruction, are alike found of each
in nature. It does not hold a principle of righteousness; it annuls the divine commandments; it
regards the divine judgment as a remote event;

it is not, in its own phrase, congenial with a substantial morality.

There come many ages and intervening crises in the slow and long advance of humanity before the words are realized and received: *Not here nor at Jerusalem; they that worship the Father shall worship him in spirit and in truth.*

There is in the revelation of the Christ the goal of religion and philosophy. They become one in their realization in the life of the spirit, — one in the realization in the life of humanity of truth and freedom.

The Christ becomes to man *righteousness and wisdom.*

CHAPTER IV.

THIS revelation is the revelation of God; it is from God, but primarily it is of God.

It is the divine self-revelation. In it God reveals himself. It is the revelation of his own being and will.

It is not a being which is abstract, and a will which is void of self-determination; it is a being which is real, and a will which is real and is realizing itself in the world.

All that God is he imparts, he reveals. He is no more a distant being, that man cannot approach him; he is not an inaccessible being, that man cannot find him; he is not an unknown being, but what he is he has made known.

This is not the revelation of an abstract universum, which then is apprehended only as the collocation of the transient forms of the finite world; it is not an indeterminate something in us not ourselves; it is not an unknown, to which the continuous and ultimate relation of man, or of a being like man, must be one of nescience; but what God is he has made known to man.

The revelation of God in his personality, in

6

his spiritual being and spiritual relations, is not of and in the physical process of the world. The physical process is the other than the spiritual, and in its relation with God is only known through the mediation of the spirit, and its characteristic is that it is constantly passing and is to pass away. It is the transient, the finite, that seems always, in its unrest and advance, to be striving to reach the infinite. There is in this revelation the recognition of the finite limitations of nature, and of the conflict in nature, as it bears in itself the reconciliation of the spirit.

There are, in the process of the physical world, the signs and the correspondences with the revelation of God, but they have the characteristic of the finite in its transience. There are signs as of beauty in the flower and of light in the sun, but it is with unceasingly passing forms, as with the flower that fades and the sun that sets. There are signs of deeper significance, as in the relations of a father and son and brother, and these are existent in the physical process of the world, but are taken up and transmuted through the mediation of the spirit, and have an ethical actualization in the moral order of the world. Thence, in the development which brings to time increasingly its fullness, there is the revelation of God and his righteousness in the moral order of the world. But this order in the family and the nation is other and higher than the physical process of the world.

This is the revelation of one who was before all worlds; who says, before the foundations of the world were laid, — *I am;* but it is not the revelation of one who is in identity with the physical process of the world.[1] It is the revelation of God in his separateness from the world, before the reconciliation of the world unto himself; it is the revelation of God in his distinctness from humanity before the manifestation of his oneness with humanity. In the physical process there is sequence, but there is not progress; there is necessity, but there is not freedom. In the historical process there is progress and there is freedom, however slow may be the development, — but that is in the life of the spirit. Thus necessity is transmuted into freedom, and sequence becomes progress. The process of the physical

---

[1] " We have a revelation in our own nature. On this revelation the church of the future must establish its claims to acceptance." (Gould, *Origin and Development of Religious Belief*, vol. ii. p. 10.) This is not strictly true. It is not strictly in our nature; it is of God, in the Christ, the Son of God who has become the Son of man, and in the relation of the Christ with humanity, and through the mediation of the Spirit; and on this the Church is built.

This is not the revelation of one who is in identity with nature, but this is the revelation of God, who is one in the final realization of the ideal with nature, — not one with the process where all forms are transient through their subjection to conditions of time, but one with nature in the realization of the perfect reconciliation.

For this conflict is not the evidence of a dualism, though of itself it would be, and in nature through the physical process there is no evidence of reconciliation. But this reconciliation is revealed, and working in and through all things; it is the revelation of God *reconciling the world unto himself.*

world is that of necessity; this does not preclude the will; the antithesis is not between necessity and freedom. While the act of sheer necessity is in itself unfree, there is an element of necessity in the freedom of the will. This element is taken up and transmuted, to use again the illustration drawn from society, as the will of man in the beginnings of its freedom and in every advance toward freedom recognizes its oneness with law: the state has its advancement in the oneness of law with liberty, and in the institution and recognition of law liberty may be attained. This physical and historical process does not, therefore, in the least preclude the will of God, in whom is perfect freedom, by whom all things subsist, and from whom all things proceed, and to whom all things come, — whose will in its self-determination has its perfect realization, from manifesting itself in the coming of the kingdom of the spirit, in which the normal course is disclosed in its end, in the coming of life out of death, and in the realization of the perfect freedom of man.

The struggle which goes on in nature is carried up into the spiritual. Thus the ascent of man and his advance is through conflict, in the realization of an ideal end in freedom; and that which is animal in its impulse and is reckless of any relation beyond its own advancement is overcome, and this struggle through its transmutation into the conflict and endeavor of man toward the perfect self-realization is ennobled. Thus in literature, as the representation of human experience, in the adventure of the Odyssey of Homer and in the progress of the Pilgrim of Bunyan, there is something more and other than the mere struggle for existence.

This revelation is its own witness.[1] It bears in itself its evidence, and the elements from which it is to be apprehended. It is not dependent upon that which is other than itself for its authentication. It is light itself, and not a refraction of something apart, that from thence it should become known. It has no need of certain criteria for its verification, which are to be adduced to enable its recognition. Revelation, as Rothe says, " springs immediately from itself."

Revelation is light. It does not need that which is apart from itself to throw an illumination upon it. It has the self-evidencing nature of light. In the physical condition vision implies only light and an organ adapted to the light.

This revelation is for another. In it is involved the relation of being for another. It has its inception in love, and is the expression of

---

[1] " In the Christian revelation it is revealed what God is; he is no more on the other side, — an unknown, — for he has made known to man what he is, and not merely in an external history, but in the consciousness." (Hegel, *Philosophie der Religion*, vol. ii. p. 191.)

the love of God and the fulfillment of the will of God toward man. It is the revelation of God to man.[1]

This revelation of God to man may be modified and limited by that in and through which it is given. The revelation which could be conceived in the physical process would be dim and transient, it would be ephemeral in comparison with the revelation in and through the life of the

---

[1] This is the truth which in one form is implied in and underlies the profound distinction of philosophy, — the distinction of being with self, and being for another, and being for self. But these adverbial terms are merely the technical phrases of philosophy. By being with self is meant being shutting itself up with itself, pursuing only its own self-aggrandizement, recognizing only a law of selfishness; being for another is not simply to subserve the uses and ends of another, — it goes forth toward another, its life is in and with another; and this is involved in being for self, which is the perfect self-realization. In this and in the subjection of the lower self, the being with self, and in the manifestation of being for another, is the perfect self-realization. It is the being with self which is the source of evil, of isolation and pride, and at last comes to know its own nakedness and poverty. It is this which is the mere assertion of a law of selfishness. This distinction is summed up in the words, *He that seeketh his life shall lose it, and he that loseth his life shall find it.* It has its justification in the ethical development of the family and the nation, where in being for another there is being for self, the realization of self.

This underlies all the contradictions which have been advanced in the recent notions of egoism and altruism, and the crude assertions of enlightened self-interest as a law of human activity.

Thus, also, in the higher development of the family and the nation man is brought nearer to God, and into a fuller knowledge of the being and love of God. It is thus, also, that, apart from the family and the nation, the hope is very faint, for the individual, of moral improvement and moral reformation.

spirit. The manifestation within the conditions and relations of the finite must be limited by these conditions and relations. The manifestation in external history must be also subject to the precedent forms of history. The revelation to man in the consciousness, the revelation in the life of the spirit, is above the limitations of the finite, and has elements that are not determined in its conditions.

This revelation is of and to a person. It is continuous; it is of and through the fullness of time. The name in the common forms of thought is the sign of the reality : this name is the name of the one of might, the Almighty, the I am, the Eternal ; it is the strong one, the holy one ; it is, as it is borne through history, the name of the Lord of Hosts. It is the name of God as one in common with men.

This revelation is not an appeal simply and immediately to an intuition, and it does not act through that alone as its organ. It is a revelation through reflection; through the pure forms of thought; through faith ; through experience ; through the life of the spirit.

This revelation is not of an abstract system, nor of certain propositions which convey certain abstract truths. It is not the presentation of certain

abstract notions about God. It is not the revelation of a scheme of divinity that man is to receive in the place of God. It is the revelation of
God himself; it is the revelation of God himself
to man. It is not the communication of a statement. It is not the exposition of that which is
only provisional and is relative to man.[1]

This revelation is not spectacular. It is not a
pageant unfolded as in the shifting changes of
some scenic movement; it is not a series of pictures. It is not the unveiling before man of that
which is always external to him, although it is a
revelation from God, in his distinctness from man,
to man, and in the manifestation of his oneness
with man. It is not a series of events, as an ad-

---

[1] Hegel uses constantly the term religion, but he is involved in
confusion in defining its relation to philosophy; he could not, while
assuming the identity of religion with the revelation of the Christ,
avoid subjecting himself to the charge of placing philosophy above
religion. But his whole conception of Christianity is merged in that
of revelation. The outline which he presents has a very high value,
and as always in this threefold distinction one clause is not to be detached from another, but each is interpenetrated by the other. This
revelation, which is positive and given to man, becomes in its realization in the life of the spirit, the life of truth and freedom.
    Hegel says : —
    " The absolute religion is —
        " (a.) The revealed religion.
        " (b.) The positive religion, as revealed to man, or a reve-
            lation to man from without.
        " (c.) The religion of truth and freedom."
                (Hegel, *Philosophie der Religion*, vol. ii. p. 60.)

vent and judgment, which pass before man, as if
man had no concern with them. It is not simply the bringing relatively nearer to him of that
which was relatively remoter from him. It enters
into and becomes the centre and the foundation
of the real life of man; or, more strictly, it is the
discovery of the only centre and foundation of
the real life of man. This revelation is of the
divine relations of the life with man. It is given,
not as the selective attainment of intellectual pursuits, nor the fruit of an exclusive culture. *I
thank thee, O Father, Lord of heaven and earth,
because thou hast hid these things from the wise
and prudent, and hast revealed them unto babes.*
It is not the reserved inheritance of the wise and
prudent, to be held as their private interest and
for their private ends. It is the revelation of
the divine fullness; it has no limitations; it is
from God, and, — as of the father in the parable,
— *Son, thou art ever with me, and all that I have
is thine.*

This revelation is through relations. It is of
the Father and the Son; it is the revelation of
that knowledge which the Son has of the Father;
its centre is in the relation of the Father to the
Son; *all things are delivered unto me of my Father,
and no man knoweth the Son but the Father,
neither knoweth any man the Father save the Son,
and he to whomsoever the Son will reveal him.*

This revelation is of a spirit and to a spirit. There must be that in man which is to receive this revelation. There can be no revelation to stones and trees and stars, nor of the spiritual to the physical. God is a person, and the revelation of God is of a person to and with a person. It thus presumes a ground of communion. It is a revelation to the reason and the conscience and the faith of men; but it is to and through them in their unity and correlation in man as a spiritual being, invested with power *to know the things of the Spirit.* It is not simply the complement of reason; it does not come to take up the lines of thought where the attainment of reason has left them; it is the correspondent, in their energy, of reason and conscience and faith. It is not simply brought to the critical tests of the reason and the conscience and the faith of men, as if it were something external to them, although it is and is to be verified of them, but it is their very element so that conscience has its right in it, and reason its ideal, and faith its rest, that they abide in it as their home. In its verification to the reason it becomes the strength of the will: *ye shall know the truth, and the truth shall make you free.*

It is not a revelation to faith alone, and the representation of it in this way rests on the apprehension of the mind itself after a molecular and mechanical formula as a component of certain dis

tinct and detached faculties and powers.   It does
not obliterate, it does not lull to sleep, the cogni-
tive faculties, the reason or the conscience, but it
elevates them in the realization of truth and freedom.[1]

It is not the revelation of certain mysteries
which are always to remain and be preserved as
mysteries. The Christ says of the kingdom of
God, it is *a mystery which is given to his disciples
to know;* S. Paul speaks of the gospel as *a mystery which is now made manifest.*   The presump-
tion is of a growth in knowledge and in life, with
the individual and the race, and in this which is
now made manifest no limits to knowledge are

[1] " When I ask what reason or right I have to believe that a man
who lived in Palestine eighteen hundred years ago was the Son of
God, I must discern in the history itself a truth and light which
meet the demands of my reason and conscience.

" It would be desolate if man was separated from God by an impassable barrier; if he belonged to an order of beings that was simply other than God. The only deliverance for man lies in the living
union of God with humanity, and not as an historical matter, but
an eternal spiritual order.

" Christianity, if true, must explain the true spiritual and moral
consciousness. Conscience is this fact. It is not merely part and
parcel of myself. It is the presence of the light, life, love of God,
met by a spiritual capacity in us of apprehending it. It is here, not
as a taskmaster or a spy, but as a guide, comforter, helper. This
presence dwells in each of us, connecting us with each other and all
with God.

" The Christ has passed through human life and human death,
bearing all our burdens, connected with every individual of the race,
not only by a bond of love, but a bond of relation, of brotherhood,
—a bond which can never be broken." (Erskine, *Memoirs*, p. 327.)

imposed. It places no barriers nor confines before
thought. It invites the approach to no Eleusinia.
It is concealed in no shrine, it is hid in no re-
cesses; it is veiled in no obscurities; it is invested in no gloom, whose twilight the imagination strives vainly to penetrate, only to be left
to grope among shadows. It is clothed with no
darkness to call forth some undefined dread,
where awe sinks into fear. The Christ says,
*Fear them not; there is nothing hidden which shall
not be known.*

This revelation is not a deposit, placed at the
disposal and within the disposition of a certain
corporation of men. It is not thus to be subjected
to the mutations of history. It is not liable to be
borne away, as in the fortunes of ancient war, to
some alien camps, and lodged in their cities. It
is not to be transferred, from one to another, as
the sacred fire that was guarded in pagan temples. It is not an esoteric faith, to be regarded
as the private stock or held as the exclusive possession of any man or body of men. Its revelation is through *the light which lighteth every man
that cometh into the world.*

It is a revelation of the truth, and the truth is
set forth as one with the life of God, and as ele-
mental in the life of man. Its requisition is of
truth in the inward parts. This revelation, in its

oneness with truth, invokes alike conscience and thought, and faith and love, and calls them forth to their field in the world.[1] It consists with the furthest reach of thought in its unimpeded advance, as it bears in itself the reconciliation of all things. It does not fall short; it passes on before the speculation of philosophy and the aspiration of religion. This revelation gives to philosophy its enduring strength and its immortal interest. There are no impassable barriers for thought, and no forces to bring to thought the intimation of their presence, only to baffle and elude the thought of man. And the emotion of religion is pervaded with an awe which is not obscured with dread, and has its exaltation with knowledge. It is the unfolding of that germ where from *faith grows virtue, and from virtue knowledge.* It penetrates with a life and power that has more than finite values,

> " all knowledge
> That the sons of men
> Shall gather in the cycled times."

This revelation, through all its gradual discoveries, must consist with the inquiry for truth in every

[1] " The dispensation of principles and of statutes is the same distinction that appears in the dispensation of Christ and of the angels. (*Hebrews*, i. 2.) The dispensation of Christ embraces in it a oneness with the mind of God; not merely a readiness to do his will when we know it, but a participation in his mind, so that by a participation in the divine nature we enter into the reason of his will, and do not merely obey the authority of his will.

" A phrase which corresponds to this distinction is that this is a fact, that is brought to the knowledge of man, of the course and condition of the world. It brings to the finite its true measures of value, in the presence of the infinite. It comes with light for all the depths and heights of human nature. The traces and tendencies of evil, of the forces working toward corruption and death, the struggle and the conflict of nature, and the contradictions of the world, in the limitations of the finite, — these consist with the redemption and the reconciliation, and have alone their solution in the manifestation of the infinite.[1] It must agree, in like

doctrine of centres, and not of circumferences. If I were residing with an oracular person, I should be in the condition of the Jews with regard to Moses. I should be living under a messenger certified by God. I should have my circumference determined for me. *If the Son shall make you free ye shall be free indeed.*" (Erskine, *Memoirs,* p. 145.)

[1] " When there comes to the conscience the revelation of a reconciled and reconciling God, of one who has manifested his only begotten Son, bearing the burden which we could not bear, taking away the sin of the world, all is changed. That which was sought in nothingness is found in a Father. The death of self is the beginning of a new life, of affections, energies, memories, hopes. These have their fruition in God. These realize their glory when he is revealed.

Therefore it is true, as of old, that the desire of nations is for a Christ, a Son of man; but for a Christ, a Son of man, in whom we may see the Father. Therefore it is true, as of old, that the preachers of a gospel to the Gentiles must go forth telling them that the Word who is their light took flesh and dwelt on earth, and suffered the death of the cross, and that they may be signed with the sign of his cross; but it is because the wisdom and power of God were revealed at Calvary; it is because the assurance was given there that sinful and dying men shall hereafter behold the face of God, and that his name shall be on their foreheads." (Maurice, *Sermons,* vol. iii. p. 128.)

manner, with that which is brought to the knowledge of man of the course and condition of the
historical world. If there were no strife within
and without of forces called good and evil, no
dominations and no slaveries; if there were no
assurance of a victory over the world, no suggestion of a glory that might invest humanity,
there might be no consistence with a redemption,
nor justification of a restoration and an eternal
life.

This does not imply a mere analogy of the constitution and course of nature. Analogy is only
an illustrative form of argument, and is formed
in material moulds and subject to material conditions. But the facts of this constitution and
course of nature, as they are brought within the
knowledge of the conscience and the consciousness of men, have in this revelation their recognition and reconciliation.

Revelation to man could not avail, unless man
could recognize its adaptation to his nature, to
complete it. It is to become the fulfillment of
his nature. Thus the relation of nature with God
may be manifested, not in the deflection of its
types, but in the persistence and attainment toward perfection of its types, as man through nature
is brought with the more perfect realization of the
ideal, nearer to God, in whom the ideal and the
real are one.

This revelation, in its gradual discoveries of facts

which are deeper than those that are the result of observation, brings its aid to science, which is the knowledge resultant from the observation of the phenomena of the physical world.[1] There is, then, no controversy between this revelation and science. This revelation brings to man, in the highest ranges of thought, the very postulates on which science rests, and the conditions of its advancement. This revelation bears in itself the one category of the truth. It recognizes the conditions of progress in the knowledge of the truth. It contends with ignorance and with superstition, in their extremest forms, because it recognizes not

[1] It is said that when theology says revelation science says law, and thence a conflict is assumed. This is a mere preliminary, it is superficial, as if when revelation says freedom science says law; for science, as the resultant of the observation of the physical world, does not allow freedom, and cannot get on with it, for the condition of the physical is that of necessity, and, in its limitation, it does not consist with freedom.

In this revelation is the realization of the life and freedom of the spirit. The necessary physical process is not annulled; this revelation brings a divine light to the course and conflict of the physical world, but it can be only to him that receives it.

And there is no demonstration of the being of the physical world. If one denies its being, no proof can meet the denial. It is true that man by the senses — by the physical organs — has a direct perception of the physical world, the eye sees, and it is a waste of thought to carry the subject through metaphysical speculation. But this does not demonstrate the certainty of the physical world to one who denies it. Then it is alone the spirit in man that discerns the things of the spirit. It may be said that one lives and acts on the assumption of the existence of the physical; but in a higher degree it is true that man lives and acts on the assumption of the reality o the spiritual.

only their intellectual degradation, but their moral debasement and defilement.

It acknowledges the unity and universality that are elements of the truth ; but these, while they form the conditions of science, are not the result of the observation of phenomena, nor the fruit of research. It also asserts this unity and universality beyond the apprehension of the understanding in its cognition of physical phenomena, not as embraced in the propositions of an abstract knowledge, but as attaining their realization through the reconciliation of all things in the spirit.

This revelation recognizes the facts in the spiritual life of man. It does not here and now assume in any moment the final determination of them, but it does not evade nor ignore them. In the course of the historical life of the world, the sin and the righteousness and the judgment of the world are facts. The world will not lose the conviction of them. It may make the study of its universities exclusively the physical process, until at last its study of the political life of man, of which once Aristotle and Hegel were masters, becomes the study of the physics of politics. Then the names in its memorial halls become only the record of molecular combinations, which in a disturbance of forces indicated, in the necessary and resultant process, certain ethical phenomena, but which are to disappear, leaving no wrack behind, when the earth is cold at its centre, and motion ceases with

7

the equalization of temperature.[1] This revelation
avoids and rejects no facts in the spiritual condition of the world.   It recognizes the slavery
and the emergence from slavery through the redemption of man.   It bears the burden of a sorrow which is illumined by no light of earth, but
is sustained by a joy in the midst of sorrow which
no gloom of earth can quench.

In science as the knowledge of the process of
the physical world, there is a discovery, — in that
form a revelation of that which is actual, and
science in its furthest advance becomes the
stronger ally of this revelation of God.   The
contest of each is with vice and crime, with the
manias and fevers that shatter men, with the
slavery of the world, and the forces which tend
to the division and degradation of humanity.

---

[1] It is the recent school of physical science that undermines
the postulates of science, when, consistently with its position, it
draws men within the immediate observation and induction which
it alone allows. Mr. Clifford, who brought to the physical school
a clear intelligence and a sincerity that did not evade its conclusions, says, "If we were to travel forward as we have traveled
backward in time, and consider things as falling together, we
should come to a central mass, all in one piece, which would send
out waves of heat through a perfectly empty ether, and gradually
cool down. As this mass got cool, it would be deprived of all life
and motion. But that conclusion, like the one that we discussed
about the beginning of the world, is one which we have no right
whatever to rest upon. It depends upon the same assumption: that
the laws of geometry and mechanics are exactly and absolutely
true, and that they will continue exactly and absolutely true for
ever and ever. Such an assumption we have no right whatever
to make." (Clifford, *Lectures and Essays*, vol. i. p. 224.)

This revelation comes to man with the assumption that he can know the truth, and that his destination is freedom. It apprehends him not simply as an individual, but in the attainment of the knowledge and realization of the universal. It passes beyond that conception which in the postulates of the physical world restricts his whole being to physical conditions, determining in its optimism and pessimism the theoretical equivalent of this whole.

In the progress of humanity there is the ampler revelation, the clearer recognition, of the eternal, and the realization of it in truth and freedom. As there may be an increase in the knowledge of the elements and conditions of a physical process, so there may be an advancing knowledge of spiritual life and relations. There has been no nation, but in the beginnings of its history there was the consciousness of a relation to a world which it did not conquer with its swords, and whose fruits it did not gather in its barns nor exchange in its markets. There has been none which, in the greater periods of its history, did not recognize ends whose worth had no estimate in material values, and in the crises of its history did not call for an effort for which its economists could find no rate of compensation in the wages of labor.

In this revelation there is the manifestation and realization of the divine reconciliation. In this revelation God passes judgment upon things finite, and in their relation with things infinite. The ultimate criteria of judgment are brought to the knowledge of man.

This revelation does not thus come to man in the assertion of a dominion over him. It is light that brings life, and the germination of freedom and its energies. S. Paul writes: *It is not that we have dominion over your faith, but are helpers of your joy, for by faith ye stand.* It has been said that submission to authority is a counterfeit of faith, and the witness to this revelation is not external to it, but is borne within it.

This revelation alone can satisfy humanity. It is vain to say, when one reads the pages of the literature of the world through the courses of its history, and in its higher forms, the pages of Aristotle and Kant or of Æschylus and Shakespeare, that man does not care for God, nor that he will loose himself from all thought of him or of a relation to him, or that he will hold his life wholly within the limitations of the finite. The life of man has not its perfect satisfaction in the finite. It will not rest in a detachment from relations to the infinite, nor in the assumption that God is an unknown.

This revelation gives its character to the work

of those who come with a message to men. They
are to bring that which has been given them to
bring. They are not to impose on it the limits
of their own notions, but to take heed lest their
own notions may mingle with it. It is not simply their own private stock in which they deal.
It is not to be held in their own dole, but as they
receive freely, they are to give freely. They are
not the constabulary of the truth, but the heralds
of it. They are not the ministers of religion, but
the messengers of God.

In the revelation of God, his manifestation is
limited, though it be a self-limitation, by the
forms through which the revelation is made ; as
it may be said of light that shines in the dark
that the darkness comprehends it not. In the
physical process, as there can be no manifestation
of the will in its freedom, there can be no revelation of beauty which is not in transient forms ;
there can be no revelation of that which is ethical, except in types that derive their significance
from the interpretation that man may give to
them, or the uses that he may derive from them.
Thus art can only take these types and forms of
nature, and employ them in the expression of its
own ideal. It works in them with the creative
imagination, and this gives its dignity to art,
though man, in the work of the creative imagination, while recognizing the profusion of these

types in nature, is conscious of the limitation of the material through which he himself works.

The revelation of the spirit and to the spirit is not within the limitation of finite forms. It is not limited to the things that are visible.

This revelation is not, then, simply relative, as if determined in external conditions. The truth consists with the consciousness of truth in man, the reason with the reason, the righteousness with the righteousness, in man.

All that God is he imparts, he reveals: he does not disguise himself that man may not know the absolute beauty; he does not withdraw himself that man may not know the absolute goodness; he does not conceal himself that man may not know the absolute truth.

This revelation is not simply an incident in the life of man, as a moment in the limitations of time; it is of the knowledge of the eternal; it is continuous; it is a revelation through experience and through history; it is in us; it is from God, it is of the Christ, it is the life of the Spirit.

CHAPTER V.

THE revelation of God is in the person of the Christ.

It is as a person that God is revealed to the world.

There is the manifestation of God in the Christ.

This revelation is not in any intellectual or historical form; nor in any form or order external to man.

It is not in a system or a series of propositions, in which an abstract truth is presented to man for the assent of his judgment, and on which his faith is to rest; nor is it in a process of thought through which man is to advance, as in the sequence of logic; nor in an isolated event in some detached epoch of history, which is thus made other than the common process of history; nor in an abstract law, as a code, that with a body of statutes is promulgated for the government of man; nor in the formulas of a system of ethics which is to shape the conduct of man.

This revelation is not in a life that is external to God, or external to man: it is in a life that is in relation with God and in relation with man;

it is in a life that is one with God and one with man.

It is a revelation of a life that is continuously one with God and one with man, *in the heavenlies,* to use the terms which are simplest and deepest, and are brought by an apostle into the common life of men. It is not one with God and one with man, as an incident in the circumstance of a finite condition. It is not thus determined by the limitations and subject to the measures of time and space.

There is in the revelation in the Christ the manifestation of the consciousness of perfect unity with God. This consciousness is the witness to the reality. This unity with God is not simply the product of consciousness, but is the reality, and has its evidence in the consciousness. The Christ manifests the consciousness of that unity with God, in which he was one with God before the world was, and that unity was maintained without being broken in and through the world.

There is the consciousness also of perfect unity with man. This had its process and realization in the human consciousness : this is the product of the human consciousness. It is a unity that is revealed as in the will of God before the world was; it is a unity that was manifested and maintained without being broken in and through the world. But this human consciousness of perfect unity with humanity was realized through a historical and in an ethical process in the world, while the very ground of that ethical process was the consciousness of perfect unity with God.

There is the perfect revelation of God in the Christ. It is in this Jesus of Nazareth, one who could say, *before Abraham was, I am;* it is in one who could say, in the manifestation of an eternal life to men, *and now, O Father, glorify thou me with thine own self, with the glory which I had with thee before the world was;* and again, *Father, I will that they also whom thou hast given me be with me where I am; that they may behold my glory which thou hast given me, for thou lovedst me before the foundation of the world.*

Thenceforth in his own life in the world, and through the human consciousness, there was the perfect realization of unity with humanity.

The Son of God became the Son of man. This denotes the perfect relation to God, — the perfect oneness with the Father and perfect oneness with humanity. It is the perfect and perfected relation of humanity with God which is the ground and condition of the fulfillment of the life of humanity. This name — the Son of man — does not indicate the mere incident of a life in certain human relations, in a certain place and time, as in the circumstance of the life of the individual. It is not thus measured, nor is it thus detached and circumscribed. It indicates a life in relations that are realized and fulfilled through the perfected human life of the Christ on earth in his oneness with humanity. It indicates a life that is continuous and organic. It is a life that is not simply finite, and does not end in death, which in itself is the finite in continuing, although changed, finite relations. There is through death the recognition of the infinite. The power given to the Christ has its continuous working toward its realization in the life of humanity. Thenceforth one has passed into the heavens who has a continuing relation with man, who is the brother of man, who sits at the right hand of the Father.

This term — the Son of man — is not thus the merely repeated phrase of an oriental form of thought, to appear with monotonous and unmeaning recurrence as the mere transcript of an earlier writer ; it has here other and larger uses.

It denotes his own personal life, his life on the earth ; and it denotes also his life in his oneness with humanity. It denotes a relation with humanity which is personal and universal. It is the real and continuous union and relation — the spiritual relation of the Christ with humanity.

Thus, for instance, this expression in the affirmation of a universal principle, and again of a divine life, is given in the words, *the Son of man is Lord of the sabbath.*

The term is used of him in his own life, in words that reflect the strange contrast of the life of man on this earth with every other form of life in the world of nature; *the foxes have holes, and the birds of the air have nests; but the Son of man hath not where to lay his head.*

It is used again of his own suffering with men, and with the suffering of men, and in the vision of things to come, and in contrast with an individual advancement that looks for a separate exaltation; *the Son of man must suffer many things, and be rejected of the priests and the elders and the scribes, and be slain;* and again, *let these sayings sink deep into your ears: for the Son of man shall be delivered into the hands of men. But they understood not this saying: then there arose a reasoning among them, which of them should be greatest, and Jesus, perceiving the thought of their heart, took a child, and set him by him, and said unto them, Whosoever shall receive this child in my name receiveth me, and whosoever shall receive me receiveth him that sent me.*[1]

[1] " With more confidence and earnestness I would hold fast those creeds and that catechism which the men of progress tell us that we must sacrifice to the interests of a general humanity. For the sake of that general humanity,—because I believe it is in danger of being utterly trampled upon, or of becoming a trumpery name which has no reality answering to it, — I would keep those treasures which have been intrusted to us. I can believe in a general, in a universal humanity, while I believe in Jesus Christ our Lord, who was born of the Virgin Mary, suffered under Pontius Pilate, was crucified, dead, and buried, descended into hell, rose again the third day,

The Christ entered into the common life of
men, and again made this the assertion of a universal principle ; *the Son of man is come eating
and drinking ; and ye say, Behold a gluttonous
man and a wine-bibber, a friend of publicans and
sinners ! but wisdom is justified of all her children.*

The term — the coming of the Son of man —
is used of his relations with humanity, that did not
terminate with his existence on earth, but had a
more perfect fulfillment.   It describes the advent
of the days of humanity ; the night is far spent,
and the dominations that crush the spirits of men
are being overcome and overthrown, and judgment
is manifested.   It is a day of judgment, and the
might is manifest of truth and righteousness and
freedom.   This is the divine life that is given to
men, — *the coming of the Son of man.*

The Christ charged the disciples, as they went
from the mount of Transfiguration, *tell the vision
to no man, until the Son of man be risen again
from the dead ;* and again, *when they persecute*

sitteth at the right hand of God, and shall come again to judge the
quick and the dead. I can assert that humanity in the very terms of
the creed, against those who would separate believers from the rest
of human beings, — who would exalt the *sect* of Christians against
the race which the Church of Christ, which Christ himself, represents.
But if I am deprived of this faith, the word humanity expresses
either an ideal which has never been realized, or else a sentiment
confined to a few fine people, or else the aggregate of all the sin and
suffering which is scattered over the world."   (Maurice, *Sermons*
vol. ii. p. 48.)

*you in this city, flee into another ; for verily I say
unto you, ye shall not have gone over the cities
of Israel till the Son of man be come.* It was
an event that was to take place in their day.
The Christ says again, *if any man shall say unto
you, Lo, here is Christ, or there; believe it not;
if they shall say unto you, behold he is in the
desert, go not forth; behold he is in the secret
chambers, believe it not: for as the lightning
cometh out of the east, and shineth even unto the
west, so shall also the coming of the Son of
man be.*

The days and years shall come and go, but this
coming is not the mere sequence of time. It is
not the evolution of forces determined in a
merely finite process. It shall be as the tide of
life sweeps on with its mingled change. It shall
blend with the varying circumstance of life. The
illustration of it may be drawn from the mythical
or the actual incident of history, and it may indicate only that traditional knowledge of historical events of a formal character which belonged
to the contemporary conditions of human life ; but
it becomes the illustration of a universal principle
that is to have its perfect realization. The words
are verified in the most recent ages, in the experience of men and nations, that they become no
more the figure of a remote imagery in history:
*as the days of Noe, so shall also the coming of
the Son of man be; for as in the days that were*

before the flood, they were eating and drinking, marrying and giving in marriage, and knew not until the flood came and took them all away; so shall also the coming of the Son of man be. It does not need the verification of a remote age; it is verified. It is to come as the world fares on with its toil and traffic, through its secular days: *likewise also as it was in the days of Lot; they did eat, they drank, they bought, they sold, they planted, they builded; but the same day that Lot went out of Sodom it rained fire and brimstone: even thus shall it be in the day when the Son of man is revealed.*

The same term is used of the future, as it shall come to his disciples; *and he said unto his disciples, the time shall come when ye shall desire to see one of the days of the Son of man, and shall not see it.*

The Christ, as the close of his existence on earth approaches, and his suffering and death are near, in answer to his accusers, asserts that exaltation of humanity that was to the elders and the chief priests and the scribes the deepest offense; *the elders and the chief priests and the scribes came together, and led him into their council, saying, Art thou the Christ? Tell us. And he said, If I tell you, ye will not believe. Hereafter shall the Son of man sit on the right hand of the power of God.* This is the exaltation which the Christ, through the suffering and death of man on this earth, has wrought for humanity. This is the power that is given to humanity. The Son of God became the Son of man, that man might be raised to the life of the Son of God.

The advent of the Christ, the coming of the Son of man, is not thus a short and isolated event in history, to be followed by ages and crises in human experience in which he is detached from it, and then to bring history to its close with the recurrence of the same event at a more remote time. The Christ is revealed.[1] The Christ the Son of man has come; he may be always coming; he is to come. The coming may be in the passing away of that which is old; in the doom of some inhuman system, as that of slavery, which has bound up with destruction the life of the family and the nation, and through some holy war, and in the ordination of society in the family and the nation upon enduring foundations; but — it will come to men as they follow their fortunes, as they buy and sell, and build and plant, though it may

[1] " We may admit that when our Lord says, *In such an hour as ye think not the Son of man cometh*, he gives us all and more than all the warning respecting the hour of death which preachers have ever drawn out of his words. We may conceive ourselves to be under a law of selfishness, and may act as though we had no ties and relationships to those around us: to each death, as any event, may be a coming of the Son of man, to pass into a region where we cannot escape that divine law of love which binds man and man, which binds earth and heaven together." (Maurice, *Sermons*, vol. i. p. 12.)

come with the confounding of their schemes, and
with the disturbance of their theories, and with
disaster to the plans they have framed. *Know
this, that if the good man of the house had known
in what watch the thief would come, he would have
watched, and would not have suffered his house
to be broken up ; therefore, be ye also ready, for
in such an hour as ye think not, the Son of man
cometh.*

But the courses and crises in the experience
of men and nations, as they pass, bring but an
imperfect apprehension of the coming of the Son
of man. It may with time become deeper, as
there comes breaking through the years the revelation of the life of humanity with the Christ,
— the glorified life of humanity, the appearing of
the Son of man, who sits at the right hand of
God.

The coming of the Son of man is thus always at
hand ; it is a constant motive to duty. It diverts
the thought of men from the apathy and dread of
a fatalism in which the world fares on, and from
following here and there after the signs and sig-
nals of the crises that may be. It does not ad-
journ the thoughts of men to some remote date,
some distant season, in which one shall come in
the guise of a king, in certain external relations,
to judge and rule the earth. It is represented
to those in that age, and in every age, as an event
for which they are to be ready, which may come

suddenly. It does not allow delay. The world may be concerned with that which is visible; and systems which divide and degrade men may prevail; and the force of fashion or of money, the idols of the avenue and the market, may be the object of worship in the streets of the city, so that men seek to win their prizes and to be counted in their companies; and tyrannies may chain down the spirits of men, and sects ride over them, and parties may count them as their own, to buy and sell; and lies seem stronger than the truth; and darkness may cover the land, so as to lead many of the very elect to fall away and not vainly may the words be spoken, *when the Son of man cometh, shall he find faith on the earth?* and yet — that darkness is not to quench hope, nor shut the thoughts of men within the clouds that sweep the closing horizon of earth; *in such an hour as ye think not, the Son of man cometh.*

The coming of the Son of man is in judgment on the powers which enslave and degrade man, and in the manifestation of righteousness, in the crises in the life of humanity, from which there comes forth a renewed life, in the revelation of the divine and eternal foundations of life.[1] It is

[1] "One of these great acts of retribution stood out before the apostles as the coming of the Son of man in their day. It gathered up into itself all the history of the previous world; it inaugurated the history of the new world.

"The destruction of the temple was to be the sign of the Son of man." (Maurice, *Sermons*, vol. i. p. 10.)

the triumph of righteousness in the manifestation of truth and freedom, which is not the product of the soil and climate of this earth, and is not resolved in its analysis into chemical combinations, and has not its glory in the grass that withereth and flower that fadeth, nor in the colors that empurple the skies, nor in the winds that sweep the fields of ocean. It has a divine strength through the Son of God, who brings to it that glory which he had with the Father, before the world was, — *the glory of the Son of man, who sitteth at the right hand of God.*[1]

Through the death of the Christ the limit of the finite is passed in the realization of an infinite life, and the isolation and separation of death, for humanity, is overcome. In the vision that passed before him when the hour of the powers of darkness was approaching, and he was accused and rejected of the elders and scribes and chief priests, and was to be slain as a malefactor on this earth, he said; *hereafter shall ye see the Son of man sitting on the right hand of power, and coming in the clouds of heaven.* In this way, S. John the Divine says of that life in that timeless æon, *no*

---

[1] "The Christ says, *Verily, I say unto you, there be some standing here which shall not taste of death till they see the Son of man coming in his kingdom.* The downfall of the exclusive nation was therefore an authentic testimony that a kingdom was established, which, however little the rulers of the earth might confess it, could have no meaner title than this, *the kingdom of the Son of man.*" (Maurice, *Sermons,* vol. iv. p. 141.)

man hath ascended up to heaven, but he that came down from heaven, the Son of man, which is in heaven.

The Christ thenceforth in the real and spiritual life of men is always present; it is the voice of one who saith, *I am he that liveth and was dead, and behold I am alive forevermore.*

The Son of God becomes the Son of man, that man may be brought into the Sonship of God.

The revelation of God in the Christ, his manifestation in the world, is as a person. In the Christ there was the perfect realization of personality, the self-determined One, in the Will that was one with the Infinite, with the righteous Father.

There is in personality an element that is individual, but this subsists with finite conditions and relations; it goes on with the inception and circumstance of a physical process on the earth.

There is in personality an element of unity and of universality; the realization of personality in men in its advance is thus towards the universal.

There is in personality an element that is relative. This relation for a person with a person is not and cannot be simply formal. It is a relation that is not thus between persons, but in persons. It is not, therefore, the immediate relation which exists between simple externals, nor can its mediation be simply external.

There was in the Christ the highest and fullest assertion of personality. It comes out, not alone in the words with others, *call no man master;* and again, *I call you not servants, but friends;* it is in the words, *there standeth one among you who is greater than the temple.* But beyond these come the words, *I am the light of the world;* and again, *I know whence I come and whither I go;* and again, *I am the way, the truth, and the life;* and again, *I, if I be lifted up from the earth, will draw all men unto me.*[1]

But this expression of personality is never apart from its relations. If he treads these heights of personality with perfect repose, he is not alone on them, nor lifted beyond the world. His words are, *I am in the Father, and the Father in me;* and again, *I and the Father are one.* And this realization of personality is not a relation for himself alone, but for humanity; it is being for

[1] " Through this strait gate of absolute trust in the Eternal God as a Father, when the evidence of events, the denials of men, the anguish of his spirit, contradicted the faith that he was a Son at all, — through this strait gate of absolute denial of his right to have anything and be anything apart from his Father he passed.

"Through this strait gate he was moving on to that *life* which he had with the Father before the worlds were. But in another sense he was moving to a new life, the life of manhood, which he had redeemed and reconciled. If the love of God could have been content with anything less than this redemption and reconciliation, with anything less than the imparting to men the full rights and condition of Sons of God, the Word would not have been made flesh; the life on earth which the evangelists set forth to us would not have been lived." (Maurice, *Sermons,* vol. ii. p. 292.)

another, in the fulfillment of being for self. That which he affirms of himself he affirms of those with him : *as thou, Father, art in me, and I in Thee, that they may be one in us.*[1] The perfect revelation of God must be in personality, for in self-determination, in truth to self, there is being for another, and in this relation, being for self, the perfect self-realization, which is the realization of the ethical life.

The relation of the Christ to God, of the Son to the Father, is perfect. This relation to God becomes then, in humanity, the foundation and condition of the realization of the human personality, which has its strength in its relation to God. It is not subject to accident, nor determined by the limitations of the finite, but recognizes its existence in the economy of an infinite wisdom and love. It is in man the life of the spirit, the life of freedom, which subsists in relations with God.

Thus, from the communion in human relations with the higher personality, there is strength

[1] " He is one who, because he claims to be the Son of God, abjures all separate authority. He is one with the Father; therefore he can do nothing of himself. He will not make the stones bread ; that would be a denial of his Sonship. His countenance becomes changed, for the Father's brightness shines through it. The agony of the cross is the sense of separation from the Father. Into the Father's hands he commends his spirit. The Magdalene is to tell his disciples that he is about to ascend to his Father and their Father, to his God and their God." (Maurice, *Sermons*, vol. ii. p. 290.)

and freedom. Thus, for a family and for a nation, the very names of those who are greatest, as Abraham and Isaac and Jacob, as Washington and Jackson and Lincoln, even in their human associations, become a source of strength and freedom. Their character becomes a power in the life of a people. But we are conscious how imperfect the attainment was and is here and now; and how often, in relation with men of the highest attainment, this freedom is imperfectly realized; and how with the highest it may be impaired; but it is not so with the relation of men with the Christ and in God.

This must be the very type of personality, as the one and the universal, that is perfect in the consciousness of its own self-determination and freedom, and perfect in the consciousness of its relation to God. The beginnings of life are in these relations; S. Paul says, *your life is hid with Christ in God.*

The life of Jesus in its individual characteristics, and in its situation on this earth, was a life subject to finite conditions and relations. In these limitations, it was a life in the secular process of the history of the world. It is the subject of biography.

This name, this domestic and tribal lineage, the scene and sphere of circumstance, the time and place, are of a transient character, and have the interest only of that which is transient. The occupation and the age are the accident of life.

The date of his birth, the site of the town in which he was born, of the tavern in which he was a guest, of the chamber in which he partook of the supper with his disciples, of the sepulchre in which he was laid, may be no more known. It is still only some human association that turns to them, and is not to be satisfied.

The fact which is apparent through them is that he became man, that he was born into the life of men. S. John says, *the Word was made flesh, and dwelt among us.* That he was born in destitute circumstance, that he died in the form of death provided by an imperial power for the offense of a slave, that his birth was in a house which he or his fathers did not own, that he was laid in a sepulchre which he or his fathers did not own, are the incidents which have been recorded in his life. This life was the common life of all men. His relations were with a common humanity. There was the realization of the historic life of man on this earth. S. Paul says, *He took upon him the form of a servant, and was made in the likeness of men: and being found in fashion as a man, he humbled himself and became obedient unto death, even the death of the cross.*

There is no incident to isolate him from the common life of men, and no circumstance which has the character of an external distinction. There is no event to which there can attach any tradition of external power or pomp. It is in no formal relation and circumstance that he appears in the human offices of a Prophet and Priest and King. There is for him no graduation, no ordination, no coronation, of this earth. It is the manifestation of the power of a King, but not one who would establish a dominion over men; of a Prophet, but not one who would impose upon human thought the systems of a school; of a Priest, but the sacrifice he offers is no fruit of time, and he stands before no altar that is built by men. He calls no man to a temple that shall be destroyed. The Christ says, *destroy this temple, and in three days I will raise it up; but he spake of the temple of his body.* His own person was the temple in which God would meet man, and man might meet God.

There is thus no trace in the character of Jesus that is special and exclusive in its individual and tribal qualities. The distinction based on a line of physical descent, as a child of the family of Abraham, or of the tribe of Judah, is always set aside. There was not in his life, or in the fulfillment of his work on the earth, that which brought him into identity in its separate character with a certain race or country. The life which he lived was the universal life.

This Jesus of Nazareth is the Christ of history.

This Jesus is the Christ of the Church, the Christ of man, who, being before the world was, and coming into the world, *came unto his own*.

There has often been a contrast drawn between Jesus of Nazareth and the Christ of history. The one, for instance, has been regarded as an actual person, and the other as an abstract and unrealized ideal. The one has been represented as a life of definite circumstance, and the other as indefinite and the construction of the imagination.

But the Jesus of Nazareth is the Christ of history. There is not only a perfect identity, but the character, the life of Jesus, has, in the Christ, its perfect realization. The one is involved in the other. This actual life, this human life under human conditions, is presumed in the Christ of history; and so also this fulfilled life, which is yet always in its fulfillment, this eternal life which is given unto men, is predicated in the actual life of Jesus of Nazareth.

This Jesus the Christ does not continue in the external relation with men, which denotes an individual life, subject to the conditions of time and space and their limitations. The close of that earthly life, through death, was the coming of the Spirit; and he who is one with the Spirit and one with humanity, enters through the Spirit into the life of humanity.

The Christ of history is the coming and manifestation of the Son of man. There is the realization of his oneness with humanity and in his power, *the power of the Son of man, who is seated at the right hand of God.* The Christ of history in the historic life, the real life of humanity, is therefore invested with power, and is glorified.

This Jesus the Christ is one with the Father in that relation which he had with the Father before the world was, and one with the Spirit, who proceeds from the Father and the Son.

This Jesus the Christ is one in whom the heavens are opened and the vision is fulfilled; *hereafter shall ye see heaven open, and the angels of God ascending and descending upon the Son of man.* In him is the eternal life. It is a continuous life, and in it death is overcome. The earthly life cannot be separated from the heavenly, nor the humiliation from the glorification; the conflict is one with us and the victory, the passion and the peace of God.

There are some recent phases of thought which ask an apologetic notice.

It is said that this Jesus of Nazareth came, through the influence of the tendencies of his times, and through reflection, to apprehend the idea of the Christ which was prevalent as some abstraction in the age, and then assumed the character to himself, and then, by the force of circumstances, was compelled to sustain the position which he had assumed. It is said that to this was added the impulse of religion and the devotion of a religious nature.

But there was not thus the apprehension of some abstract idea, and the effort to conform to it; nor was personality so empty and freedom so impaired as such subjection to external circumstance would involve; nor is the relation which he manifested to the will of God, and his fulfillment of it, to be construed as a subjection to the transient circumstance of an earthly condition. There was prevalent the hope and faith often confused, but never wholly lost, which was expressed by the woman of Samaria and in the confession of S. Peter, that the Christ was to come; but that divine apprehension and realization which was in his life was rejected utterly in his own generation, and has been but slowly and imperfectly apprehended through the succeeding centuries. It was not only rejected in his generation, but alone, and yet not alone, he passed through death.

It is not, again, that he in an imperfect way assumed the character, and that his friends together worked it out in an imaginative reconstruction. The mythical element, if it be allowed in the literature of the subject, consists only with the traces of certain circumstances, and does not in the main concern the actual, and still less the ethical, development. And there is no note of imaginative power, and no representation of an abstract ideal such as occupies the representative imagination. It is not, again, that in that age, or in the succeeding ages, the historical character is clothed with certain qualities by the representative imagination, and thus, apart from the real, is idealized and lifted to its exaltation through the abstract imagination.[1]

It is not the expression of an individual ideal, but it is the manifestation of a life and in relations, and it has not its end as an individual ideal in being by self. The Christ says, *I came to do the will of him that sent me;* and again, *I can do nothing alone;* and again, *I have finished the work that thou gavest me to do.* It does not borrow its exaltation from an abstract ideal, but its exaltation is in its own perfect realization. It is beyond the power of the representative imagination, and that does not contribute an element to it. It is not the incorporation of an individual ideal, and that would avoid the element which is constant in it in its relation to God and to humanity. And this abstraction of the imagination which this theory projects is not the life of the Spirit.

It is said that this is a life which did not

---

[1] "If the Christ of the church is an ideal being, it was Jesus who made the ideal. The ideal in him is simply the result of that disengagement from the earthly vestiture which death and distance work in all who live in history. A perfect portrait presents the characteristic mode, not the temporary accidents, the fallings-off, the vanishings, of the person portrayed." (Hedge, *Ways of the Spirit* p. 338.)

recognize a system of economy, and this is assumed to be the formal system of a recent school; and again that it did not contribute to the critical culture of art. But, slightly to notice this, this was not its aim or end. It was to set forth that which is at the foundation of every human life. And in the life of the spirit there is no element of grace or truth that art can mould or thought inform, and no substantial attainment of humanity in individual or social economy, in which the power of this life may not be manifest.

There has been a recent controversy as to the ethical motive of the Christ; for instance, was it faithfulness to an ideal; or conformity to a principle of righteousness; or enthusiasm for humanity? There was the realization of the truth; and the recognition of righteousness; and love for man; but there was not a separate motive thus alone or primarily, and an ethical motive was not thus external to him. There was the manifestation of a relation to humanity that was deeper than any external motive, as an enthusiasm for humanity. The motive was in the will and love that was before the world was. He came to manifest himself to the world. He came to fulfill himself in the world.

The coming of the Son of God, the incarnation, was not simply physical, a manifestation of external power, as that which has been so often assumed in history.[1] S. John says, *the Word was made flesh, and dwelt among us, full of grace and truth.* It was ethical and organic; and it was not ethical in a formal way, but in the realization of personality; and it was not simply in an individual way, but in the life that was given for man, and became the life of humanity.[2]

There is a tendency to recognize the coming of the Christ simply in its external manifestation, in history, and to look to his coming again in a formal external manifestation. This is unspiritual. It occupies the mind with an incident of history, and in a detached way. It tends to dwell upon the incident and circumstance of the life of Jesus.

---

[1] " The Christ says, run not hither and thither ; the kingdom of God is within you. Many others were honored as divine messengers or as divinities. For instance, statues were erected among the Greeks to Demetrius Poliorcites as to a god, and the Roman emperors were honored as gods. So there have been incarnations conceived, as Buddha, Hercules. But the history of Christ is history for the community, and has the witness of the spirit in the life of faith. Thus it is maintained in a spiritual way, and not by external power." (Hegel, *Philosophie der Religion*, vol. ii. p. 321.)

[2] " This notion that the divine is only the apotheosis of the human, not its ground, — that a man is to become a god by thinking himself one, — this philosophical reproduction of all that has been most corrupt, most superstitious, in the world's history, is at once the natural reaction against a theology which takes account only of man's depravity, and the natural deduction from a theology which begins from man instead of from God." (Maurice, *Sermons*, vol. i. p. 345.)

It is regressive, and does not apprehend his real presence, nor his life and coming in the world. S. Paul says, *though I have known Christ after the flesh, henceforth know I him no more.*

The Christ in his humanity and in his relation to humanity is manifested as the head of the human race, in its real and eternal life.[1] We are members one of another, but we are related in him ; and this is the ground, and thence is the manifestation of the ethical life and relations of humanity. The relation of humanity is not simply a physical relation, and through lines of physical descent.[2] There is a physical relation, and there

---

[1] This is the truth that underlies one of the most profound and affecting doctrines of philosophy, the doctrine of reminiscence in Plato. It is the consciousness, however dimly apprehended, that the soul has of its origin and relations. This has been made the subject of one of the most impressive works of this age, the Ode on the Intimations of Immortality of Wordsworth.

" Christ was the new head of the human nature. Christ is the second Adam, the real unfigurate head of the human body. He suffered death as a partaker of that life which was under the law of death, and rose again with a new life. In the person of Christ risen, then, we see God in fellowship with our nature, — even with us." (Erskine, *Memoirs*, p. 115.)

[2] " Men found continually that the further they went down into themselves the more there was of corruption and darkness and evil, till at last they supposed the very root of their being was nothing else. S. Paul had gone down into these depths; he had found this rottenness; in himself he says he found only that. But he discovered that there was a root below himself, a true divine root, for himself and every man. He found that each man, when he tries to contemplate himself apart from Christ, is that evil creature in which no good dwells. But no man, so he teaches, has a

is also a spiritual relation. Through the physical condition there is the evidence that there is no ground for the monistic representation of man. The ethical relation of man is that which gives to social law and the development of history an element that is universal. The Christ is revealed as the true and eternal head of the human race. It is the life of the Spirit; for that which is made is physical and determined through forms and with component elements, but that which is spiritual is given to men; it is, in the profound words, *begotten, not made.* S. Paul says, *the first man is of the earth, earthy : the second man is the Lord from heaven: and as we have borne the image of the earthy, we shall also bear the image of the heavenly.* The Christ is not the prefigurate, but the real, head of humanity. Thus, in history, the law which he has given becomes increasingly the law of the life of humanity, and the expression of its relations. S. Paul says, *I would have you know that the head of every man is Christ.* This is the life which is brought to light; *in him was life ; and the life was the light of men.*

The Trinity denotes, as a term, the revelation of God in himself, and in his relation to humanity. There is thus in the Trinity the assertion of the

right to contemplate himself apart from Christ; God does not so contemplate him.　He was formed at first in the Divine Word in him he lives and has his being still ' 　(Maurice, *Sermons* vol. i. p. 108.)

unity of God; but it is not an abstract unity, a unity in which there is no foundation for relations. It is not an isolation.

The term has necessarily the suggestion of formulas and systems, and with the profoundest significance it is apart from and alien to the form of expression of the Scriptures and the worship of the Church, and has no intimation of the fullness that is in the words, *the Father, the Son, and the Holy Spirit.*[1]

It contains no suggestion of the words of the Christ; of those of whom he said, *as thou hast sent me into the world, even so have I also sent them into the world. Holy Father, keep through thine own name those whom thou hast given me, that*

---

[1] This term, the Trinity, must submit to the defect which attaches to nearly all terms which from common uses are brought to the uses of a strict metempiricism. Its defect is that it brings out the mere quandary of the practical understanding, the numeration as in an arithmetical note of three and one. But this is not to be regarded when the term comes to be considered strictly as a symbol. These terms, in their derivative uses, are of more value in the Greek than in the Latin schools. The reason for this is both literal and historical. Mr. Maine has some important notes on the use of these terms in the Latin schools. (*Ancient Law*, p. 80.) "The term Trinity is a hieroglyph." (Fisher, *Faith and Rationalism*, p. 55.) Dr. Fisher has references to Dr. Chalmers and Dr. Newman, in illustration of this subject. See S. Augustine, *De Trinitate*, ii. 12.

"The Council of Nicæa, which declared the union of God with man, is one of the most important assemblies that was ever convened on this earth; it dates a new era in the history of human thought. God in actual contact with man — God in man and man in God — is the underlying idea of the Athanasian dogma, which asserts that the Son is consubstantial with the Father." (Hedge, *Ways of the Spirit*, p. 352.)

they may be one as we are.   I in them and thou in
me, that they may be made perfect in one, and that
the world may know that thou hast sent me, and
hast loved them as thou hast loved me.

In the Christ, the Son of God who becomes the
Son of man, there is the revelation of him who is
one with the Father, who, being one with the
Father, became one with man, and through him
humanity is brought into relation with God; and
there is the manifestation of the Father with the
Son, and there is the coming of the Spirit, that
the life of humanity becomes henceforth the life
of the Spirit.

The Christ Jesus of Nazareth says, with words
that could have no justification in a merely physical
process of history; *it is better for you that I go*
away, and the Spirit of truth shall come; he will
guide you into all truth, and he shall not speak
of himself, but whatsoever he shall hear that shall
he speak; he shall glorify me, for he shall receive
of mine and show it unto you.

That Jesus is the Christ, the Son of God, becomes the fact of history.   It is his departure that
is the coming of the Spirit and the life of the
Spirit: the life which has not its precedent nor its
tradition in a physical development; the life which
is not merely an object of the acquisition of the
intellect; the life which is not variable nor transient, with subjection to the limitations of time

and space, which does not return to mingle with the dust, nor yield to corruption; the life which is eternal.

The relation of the Christ with humanity has an organic character, which does not exist alone in the relations of an external history, and passes beyond the limitations of the finite, in the life of the spirit. There was a repose and a knowledge of things to come that was not of this earth in the words; *it is better for you that I go away.* The voice that again broke the silence was not of this earth; *Lo, I am with you alway, even unto the end of the world.*

This going away was his coming again in the realization of infinite and eternal relations, in the life of the spirit. If the Christ had remained continuously on the earth, it would have been necessarily in an external relation, a relation limited by time and space. It is the fact of his going away, and thenceforth the coming of the Spirit, in the real life, the immortal life, of men, that becomes the evidence of the divine presence and the divine character, and thence transfers the evidence to history. It is here that the skepticism of men is to meet it. It will not be found by running to and fro, and vainly they may listen to voices that say lo here and lo there. It will not verify itself by external pageants. It will verify itself through the life of the Spirit in the history of the world; and as the skepticism of men must meet it there, so the faith of men shall there have its strength, and thence shall come the sources of an undying life.   He says, *if any man confess me before men, him will I also confess before the face of my Father in heaven.*[1]

That Jesus is the Christ, the Son of God, has henceforth the evidence of the Spirit.

There is henceforth the life of the spirit.   This is the life that now is and is to come.   This is the life of truth and freedom ; in this man overcomes the world ; the fruition of it is righteousness and peace and joy.

There is henceforth the conviction of the world.

There is henceforth the realization of the kingdom of heaven on the earth.

There is henceforth the redemptive life of humanity.

There is the life in which death is overcome, — the life of the spirit.

---

[1] The question which the contemporaries of the Christ asked has been repeated in other ages, and by many in this age, " What sign showest thou unto us ? "   The most significant fact in that age for those who asked this question, then, was the destruction of the temple, and the coming with the new testament of that spirit which dwelt in men.   S. John says, *the Jews said unto him, What sign showest thou unto us ? Jesus said unto them, Destroy this temple, and in three days I will raise it up.   Then said the Jews, Forty and six years was this temple in building, and wilt thou raise it up in three days ?   But he spake of the temple of his body.*

CHAPTER VI.

THERE is through the world the conviction of sin, of righteousness, and of judgment. The course of the sin of the world is in its alienation and separation from God, and consequent variance and strife. This condition, which appears in the manifold forms of rebellion, of envy, of division, of violence, is a constant fact in the history of the world. In this separation from God is the want of unity and reconciliation and peace. In this, is the source of those false theories of dualism which always involve fatalism, and against which the spirit of man, in its aim toward unity, contends with unconquerable energies. In this, man's life becomes one with nature in its continuous course, but does not rise above it. It is simply an animal existence. It is one with nature as the other of God. In this, there is no freedom. There is no recognition of the ground of unity and reconciliation, as it is found through the mediation of the spirit.

Sin is the alienation of man from God and from humanity, through the assertion of the law of selfishness as the final law of human action. S. Paul says, *sin is the transgression of the law.* It is a transgression by man of the law which is the law of his own being, — the law of God and of humanity. It involves a variance from the relations of men in their true and normal development, and from the moral constitution of the world, and consequent injury and consciousness of guilt. Sin consists in following ways that are wrong, as in a wrong world, and in rejecting or refusing the recognition of a law or life of righteousness. Through it the will is unfree,[1] and is brought into subjection to that which is external, and injury may be done to others in their relations in life. In sin there is the defect and the defeat of personality. It is a malady by which hurt is done

---

[1] " From the internal point of view there are rudiments and survivals in the mind which are to be excluded from *that me,* whose free action tends to progress; that *baneful strife which lurketh* inborn in us is the foe of freedom : *this let not a man stir up, but avoid and flee.*" (Clifford, *Lectures and Essays,* vol. ii. p. 250.) This is presented not only as the result of experience, but as the resultant of the knowledge of human nature derived from observation. There can be in one way no more clear and incisive description of human sin. The phrase, which will hold its place on historical grounds, as descriptive of those forces which hinder from action *that me,* is *the bondage of sin.* Whatever may be our theories, the science of theology asks no more than to be supplied with these postulates; and it may hold that something deeper, yes, diviner in *that me,* may be traced beneath rudiments and survivals; and still sin is *alien* to man, as it is an *alienation* from God, and that *baneful strife which is a foe to freedom,* which man is to avoid and flee, is another conflict than the struggle for existence on this earth, and out of it is that freedom wrought, which is fulfilled in a life that does not have its consummation in death.

to man, and is the disruption of the normal relations of society. The true development of man is thwarted.

Sin is involved with ignorance in a world of finite conditions. Sin is incident to this imperfect condition and development, in which man may rise above the mere courses of an animal existence, through the mediation of the spirit, and evil may be overcome through conflict; and this present evil world is brought into reconciliation with God through the spirit; and this divided world is stayed in the centre of its unity in God; and peace is attained in the recognition and the fulfillment of the will of God.

In sin there is the isolation of the individual; self is an object of action, not in truth for self, — for in truth for self, there is the realization and recognition of a relation to God and to humanity, — but in being with self, the mere living of a man unto himself, the assertion of a law of selfishness. Thus the words are verified, —

> " This above all, to thine own self be true;
> And it must follow as the night the day,
> Thou canst not then be false to any man."

There is in the sequence of the physical process the isolation that is death. In death there is isolation, and an extinction of being in the relations of life, and an effacement of structural forms in which these relations had their continuance in the process of the physical world. S. Paul says, *the sting of death is sin.*

It is this separation in death against which the spirit in man protests, and this isolation of death from which the heart of man shrinks, with forebodings of dread and gloom. There is in death also the apparent limitation of man to the physical process of the world, and entire subjection to that process.[1] It is through disease and death in the physical process that there is the prostration of man. The science of man recognizes these facts, which appear in forms of disease and death, and as involving not merely deflection from the type, but in the individual the extinction of the type; it is not simply a replacement in the evolution of forms, but it is displacement. The inference from the physical process in its limitations is that disease, with its pain and anguish, is to be apprehended as normal. Man can ascertain, in the widest range of observation, no period in which disease, with pain and anguish, has not existed through identical forms of life, and, inferentially, none in which it will not exist. He can indicate no period in which disease, with pain and anguish and death, will disappear, and no type of physical organization with which it will disappear. And

[1] It is true, in the profound words of Spinoza, that the free man thinks of nothing less than of death, — *homo liber de nulla re minus quam de morte cogitat ;* but this is true because freedom has an infinite quality, and is not measured in the limitations of the finite; and in freedom man is raised above the mere limitations of the finite. But the school of physical science does not know this, and cannot admit this, without the rejection of its own assumptions. The facts concerning death are within the range of its observation.

this evolution may have shortly or remotely a devolution, — this gradation may become a degradation.

There is in sin the subjection of man, as there is subjection in the physical process to death. The spirit of man recognizes the fact that sin is privative and positive, but it is not positive in the sense of affirmation of being; it is external and spiritual, but it is not spiritual in the sense of the recognition or realization of life. Sin is the bondage, the slavery of men. The freedom of man fails of its realization, and man becomes the slave of sin.

Sin is common, and is not restricted to a certain individual or a tribe; it attaches to the race; it refers to each individual, to each family and nation, and through it their strength and freedom are impaired. Through sin the life of each is deflected from its real end, and perverted from that consistence which is in truth to self; and its action, when its self-determination, that is, its freedom, is gone, becomes wayward and weak, as of one that is lost.

The fact of human sin is recognized by the conscience and the consciousness of men and nations. It has its evidence in their history. There has been no greatness in men or in nations, in Greece or in Rome, that achieved a complete exemption from this consciousness. It is attested in the literature of the world, and most clearly in its highest forms, as in the Odyssey of Homer, the Æneid of Vergil, in Æschylus and Shakespeare.[1]

And when once the conscience and the consciousness of men has awakened to the sense of sin, with discord and death, there comes for it no obliteration. There is found in the changes of place and time no river of oblivion. When once it has been aroused, —

> " Nor poppy, nor mandragora,
> Nor all the drowsy syrups of the world,
> Shall ever medicine thee to that sweet sleep
> Which thou owedst yesterday."

And as there is here no power that can bring to the conscience the effacement of sin, so there is in the physical process no power to overcome and destroy death. Nature says, It is not in me; she brings forth, in the same indifference, life and death; she weaves of the same texture the wedding garment and the shroud. And natural society says, It is not in me; she has obtained the occupancy of no land where, through avarice and

---

[1] " Poor soul, the centre of my sinful earth,
Fool'd by those rebel powers that thee array,
Why dost thou pine within, and suffer dearth,
Painting thy outward walls so costly gay?
Why so large cost, having so short a lease,
Dost thou upon thy fading mansion spend?
Shall worms, inheritors of this excess,
Eat up thy charge? is this thy body's end?
Then, soul, live thou upon thy servant's loss,
And let that pine to aggravate thy store;
Buy terms divine in selling hours of dross;
Within be fed, without be rich no more:
So shalt thou feed on death, that feeds on men,
And death once dead, there's no more dying then."

(Shakespeare, *Sonnets*, cxlvi.)

violence, she has not consumed the lives of her children; she has the records of no age that is exempt from the follies and crimes and wars of men.

The fact of sin is recognized, by the struggle for survival in the conditions of life; by the variance from the ideal in the secular succession of things in men and nations; by the civil procedure and institutions of society; by the language of men, which may be held as representative, not of its lower, but of its common condition. That in language there is retrospectively a discovery of man to himself, and that this civil procedure is in the institution of a moral order is simply the evidence of tendencies and forces that are brought to act in conflict with evil.

Sin is the transgression of the law, the law of being, in which one *wrongeth his own life*. It is followed by evil. This is indicated in the civil order of society, which has not alone a positive, but a substantial ethical ground. Crime is punished. This punishment is the manifestation of the crime. This illustrates the conviction which increasingly follows sin.

Sin is the contradiction of life. In sin man is, himself, in contradiction with all that really is. It is not only the subversion of energy, but it becomes the identification with the unreal. It is the movement of an empty masquerade. The actor says in that awful tragedy, —

"I 'gin to be aweary o' the sun."

This, in human experience, is the unreality of sin, that, in the gathering night yet discerns through the baleful shadows, its own discord. This becomes its intolerable burden and its ceaseless torment; in the fable, it was the whip of scorpions.

Sin is unreal; — it is the contradiction of life; but in the consciousness of its contradiction there is the evidence of a deeper unity, in which it may be overcome, and of the ground of its obliteration. There may be a root of righteousness of life that is deeper than the root of evil. Though it be not our discovery, it may be discovered to us. The conviction of sin may come with the conviction of righteousness and with the discrimination of evil, in the judgment, that is, the coming of the light.

The Christ says of the coming of the Spirit, *And when he is come he will convince the world of sin, of righteousness, and of judgment: of sin, because they believe not on me; of righteousness, because I go to my Father, and ye see me no more; of judgment, because the prince of this world is judged.*

There is the manifestation of God in the ethical order of the world. There is the manifestation of the will in the assertion of law, in the fulfillment of righteousness, and in the realization of freedom.

The ethical process of the world is in the development of the family and the nation. In this there is the maintenance of relations, and the institution of rights and the acknowledgment of duties in which freedom is realized. Through the conscious life of men and of nations there is the recognition and the realization of righteousness and freedom.

The ethical process of the world is the fulfillment of the life of humanity. The degradation of man is overcome, and men are lifted above a brutal condition, with its ignorance and servility. It raises man above the existence which is merely animal, the situation which has its satisfaction through the acquisition of enough for its animal desires.

This revelation is of a God of righteousness, who will establish righteousness on the earth. The law of righteousness is to have its vindication in the relations of men. This has in history its constant assertion. It is borne on in one continuous strain, with voices of joy that proclaim the assurance of deliverance, as in the exultant anthem of a mighty nation, and voices that are tremulous with the burden of woe: *Righteousness exalteth a nation;* and again, *in the way of righteousness is life; as the whirlwind passeth, so is the wicked no more, but the righteous is an everlasting foundation.* The same ethical expression is in the opening services of the Church: *when the wicked man turneth away from his wickedness that he hath committed, and doeth that which is lawful and right, he shall save his soul alive.* The very word righteousness is a constant term of the Old Testament, *O ye that love the eternal, see that ye hate the thing that is evil! to him that ordereth his conduct right shall be shown the salvation of God.*[1] It is repeated with no limit in its universal significance, *all flesh shall know that I am thy Saviour and thy Redeemer.* It is blended with the vision of its transcendent hopes; *this is the name whereby he shall be called, the Lord our righteousness.* The highest reward is for him that *loveth righteousness and hateth iniquity.*

The assertion and recognition of righteousness is in and through the conscience. The conscience is not alone the expression of an external and formal law, although the affirmation of the conscience may be in an external and formal law; it is in a law which is involved in the being and freedom of personality — I, I ought.[2]

---

[1] " The word righteousness is the master word of the Old Testament. *Keep judgment and do righteousness! Cease to do evil, learn to do well.* A sentence which sums up the New Testament, and assigns the ground on which the Christian church stands, is this: *Let every one that nameth the name of Christ depart from iniquity.*" (Arnold, *Literature and Dogma,* ch. i. 2.)

[2] " He who, wearied or stricken in the fight with the powers of darkness, asks himself in a solitary place, ' Is it all for nothing? Shall we, indeed, be overthrown?' he does find something which may justify that thought. In such a moment of utter sincerity, when a man has bared his own soul before the immensities and eternities, a presence in which his own poor personality is shriveled into nothingness, arises within him, and says as plainly as words can say, ' I am with thee, and I am greater than thou.'' (Clifford, *Lectures and*

The revelation of God is in the fulfillment of righteousness and the realization of freedom. In righteousness and freedom is the assertion and realization of personality.

The conscience of man presumes the being of God; it presumes a righteous being. There can be no adequate apprehension of conscience, nor explanation of the facts of conscience, — to consist with the facts given in the human consciousness, — that does not imply the being of God, and his relation to man.

The conclusions of conscience are not simply the result of certain physical processes and conditions, and determined by the application through them of some law or standard of convenience or use.

The principle of right or of righteousness has not its origin in a physical process, which in transmitted lines of descent allows no real freedom, and is determined only by immediate considerations of advantage or disadvantage.

It has not its origin in customs, as a usage which might be wholly different in different conditions, nor requires from men only a conformity to prev-

Essays, vol. ii. p. 242.) It may not concern one what name, of many names, is given to this presence, if it be not a mere word for which there 's no reality, and if it be not merely identified with the ephemeral life of humanity; if it be a presence in and with personality; and if the personality of man be not brought to nothingness, but lifted up, from among the things which pass into nothingness, into strength and freedom.

alent customs as those, for instance, of a tribal or racial character.

It has not its origin in a simple intuition, for it presumes that which is the object of intuition; and while there may be a certain intuitive apprehension of righteousness, yet it is more often brought to the knowledge of men through reflective lines of thought.

It has not its origin in considerations of utility, as the relative advantage or disadvantage of certain courses of action as tending to promote an individual or tribal welfare.

And yet there is a truth involved in each of these notions, for a principle of righteousness is recognized in that custom, which men with the advance of a civil polity respect, as a ground of customary right and of common law; and it may be apprehended by the intuition of thought; and it may be ascertained through experience and trial with the sequent issues of good and evil in the process of society.[1]

[1] "Marriage was an institution far older than the law. It was not the creation of the law.

"The morality of the Pharisees proceeded upon the forgetfulness of this principle. They looked upon penal laws not as presuming obligations, but as the foundation of them." (Maurice, *Sermons*, vol. ii. p. 350.)

Mr Clifford has a theory of morality: "This theory is the theory of the tribal self, or the partly inherited partly acquired sense of what the good of your clan requires, which must often be at war with what your own individual pleasure seems to require, — the conflict representing the emergence of conscience." See *Lectures and Essays*, vol. ii. p. 113. This is a fact in human nature, which any theory

The principle of righteousness is absolute ; it is immutable ; it is universal.

This principle is involved in the realization of the life of the family and the nation. It is not within their option to determine whether it shall or shall not be. It had not its origin in the assertion of any individual or collection of individual men, and it cannot be annulled by them. It is the source of stability, —

> "The most ancient heavens
> Through thee, are fresh and strong."

That there is a course and constitution of human nature, that there is an ethical process involved in the relations of men, that righteousness has for its consequence life and freedom, that unrighteousness has its consequence in the detriment of life and subversion of freedom, — this is the evidence of the presence of a righteous being in the ethical process of the world.

of the evolution or education of the world does not affect. But is this conflict of the whole and the individual, or of the tribal self and the separate self, always to go on; and if in the sacrifice of the individual self there be an element of virtue, may there not be, in the old words, a divine or eternal law or ground of sacrifice, deeper than the mere contingent conflict of one man and a group of men ; and in this process of virtue, with the " emergence of conscience," does a man become a mere underling or is there a higher realization of the individual self, — the me, — as through this process it rises to the universal, and is there thus the way to a perfect reconciliation ? This fact, of the deepest import, has its perfect vindication and justification in the Christian ethics, and involves elements other than a mere impulse, toward " an end in which we are all to be swept away in the final ruin of the earth."

10

There is a revelation in righteousness of the being of God to the world. This revelation is to and through the conscience and the consciousness of men.

This is not an abstract righteousness, nor a formal freedom. There is in personality the highest energy; the assertion of that energy is in freedom.

The energy which works in freedom is, through conflict, in the realization of personality. But this is not, as in the struggle for existence in the physical process, the struggle of one against another, with the resultant survival of one by another, but the struggle where each, in their relations, is for another, and each in the realization of righteousness and freedom is for all.

This righteousness in its assertion and realization is more and other than a retributive or distributive justice, which is the postulate of the schemes of a formal theology: its revelation becomes in the unity of the ethical process and life the consistence of truth and goodness and beauty, and the ground of faith and hope and love in humanity. It does not allow that ethical incongruity which has for its postulate a conflict of justice and love, that requires a formal and external reconciliation.

The perfect manifestation of righteousness is in the person of the Christ. The law of righteousness is not abstract; — it is manifested in the realization of personality, and in the life and relations of men in the world. It is in a life in which there is the consciousness of perfect unity with God and perfect unity with man, and which becomes in itself the perfect realization of the truth.

The life of Jesus the Christ was not simply a sinless life, with the negative quality, that it was without sin. It was that, but it was of a positive ethical quality. It was not alone the representation, the mere bodying forth of a perfect ethical character, a phenomena of excellence, a simular of virtue, but it was the manifestation of a life in the realization of a perfect righteousness in perfect unity with man. It was a life that was wrought through the trial of earth, in the realization of righteousness. It was a real conflict and a real victory.

In the life of the Christ there was the fulfillment of the law. The Christ says, *I came not to destroy, but to fulfill the law.* The apostle says, *it became him to fulfill all righteousness.*[1]

[1] " The gospel perfects, fulfills, completes the law. The lawgiver who deals with acts says: *Thou shalt not kill.* The king who speaks to the heart says, *Thou shalt not be angry with thy brother without cause.* The lawgiver who deals with acts says : *Thou shalt not commit adultery.* The king over the spirit who speaks to the heart says, *Thou shalt not look upon a woman to lust after her.*

" The gospel is therefore, from the foundation, necessary as the law itself to the perfect development of humanity.

"Jesus could raise the standard of human morality in opposition to the inhuman standard which the Pharisee set up, because he was himself the Son of man; because he came to declare, and in his own person to manifest, the truth that God and man are not divided, but

It does not take away one jot from the law. It does not abrogate the commandment; it is to exceed the righteousness of the scribe and Pharisee. It does not annul the principle of an eye for an eye, — it retains it, but it transmutes it; it retains the law, — it does not render it void, it transmutes it. It is raised to the conception of a spiritual ethic. It becomes not simply the observance, but the fulfillment, of the law. It is no longer external and formal as the discipline of a school master, as of those of old time. It is not simply the precedent of the scribe nor the maxim of the Pharisee.[1] It is spiritual, and is to become the law of the life and freedom of the spirit. It is no longer simply a command, *thou shalt* and *thou shalt not*, although this persists, but it adds *and further, thou shalt love;* and it comes to the individual as existing in divine relations, and in an ethical life in which the goodness of man is one in its quality with the goodness of God, *be ye perfect, even as your Father which is in heaven is perfect;* as the divine forgiveness is a rescript of our forgiveness, *forgive us our trespasses as we*

eternally united; because, therefore, that which is truly human must answer to that which is truly divine." (Maurice, *Sermons*, vol. ii. p. 350.)

[1] "We do not know our duties apart from our relations, and the knowledge of our relations helps us to the performance as well as the knowledge of our duties." (Erskine, *Memoirs*, p. 344.) "I know no ground for the relationships among men but their common relation to God." (Maurice, *Sermons*, vol. i. p. 15.)

forgive those that trespass against us. It is not a local nor an exclusive morality, but it is a universal morality; — *that ye may be the children of your Father which is in heaven ; for he maketh his sun to rise on the evil and on the good, and sendeth rain on the just and on the unjust.*[1]

The ethical principle has in every form a constant affirmation. It is the law of judgment and of life. The Christ says, *if thou wilt enter into life, keep the commandments ;* and again, *if ye love me ye will keep my commandments.* S. Paul says, *be not deceived ; God is not mocked ; for whatsoever a man soweth that shall he also reap ; for he*

[1] "The morality of the gospel, because it proposes to man only the highest standard, lays less burden upon him than any other. The Christ teaches us that the burden is not in the straitness of the law, but in ourselves; that a law, every law, human or divine, must be weak through the flesh; that so long as we are merely trying to obey a rule we shall find that rule a burden; that when we claim our rights as new men, as created in Him to good works, as children of a Father in heaven, we become united with Him from whom laws proceed. Obedience to them is recognized as part of our constitution; disobedience is the unnatural, miserable state.

"If this morality of the Christ is not casuistical morality, still less is it rhetorical morality. The rhetorician exalts virtues, as if they were characteristic of certain favored persons whom it is his calling to praise; denounces vices, as if none could have fallen into them but those whom it is his calling to vituperate. Our Lord speaks of the highest virtues which any man has ever practiced as being resemblances to the Father in heaven, who has made all men in his image; who has redeemed all in Christ, that they may be renewed in his image. Our Lord treats all vices which the law condemns as lying close to every man, as being the consequences of inclinations to which no man is a stranger." (Maurice, *Sermons*, vol. ii. p. 343.)

*that soweth to his flesh shall of the flesh reap cor-
ruption; but he that soweth to the Spirit shall of
the Spirit reap life everlasting.* The law is universal; whatever be the schemes or theories of men,
it is continuous and invariable. It is not annulled
through faith, but through faith there may come
a deeper knowledge of its reality, — of that corruption which shall say unto the grave, Thou art
my mother! and of that life which is unto the
spirit, and of the spirit shall reap life everlasting.
But the law is invariable, as a man soweth so
shall his reaping be.

The revelation of God and of his righteousness
is in the judgment of the world. It is the judgment of men and of nations.

This judgment is the revelation of light. It is
a day of judgment; it is the day of the Lord as
the prophet saw it; it is the day of the coming
of the Son of man.

It is a judgment of righteousness. It is not an
event; it is a crisis. It is not retired to a remote
past; it is not adjourned to a more remote future.
It is a judgment whose hour is not thus known to
those to whom it comes, in the crises of human
existence. It is not merely an event in the sequence of affairs, — it is a judgment with the
discrimination of good and evil and the issue of
righteousness. It is not of one day or one age
alone ; it is here and now. The Christ says, *now*

is the judgment of this world; and in that transcendent vision, *I beheld Satan as lightning fall
from heaven.*

This judgment is an object of desire. The patience with which the forces of wrong and fraud,
the evil of the world, is endured is with the conviction that a day of doom shall come. The
prayer thus has always been, *Arise, O Lord, and
judge the earth.* Through the ages it has been
repeated, *Let the earth rejoice, for he cometh in
righteousness to judge the world, and the people
with his truth.*[1]

The man of affairs, the statesman whose ethical
conception does not consist with the material systems and commercial theories of recent schools,
has said that what he dreaded for his land was
not the day of judgment, but the day of no judgment.

This judgment is itself grounded on the principle which it makes known; that human life has
not its origin nor its completeness in the limitations of a physical process; that we live in infinite
relations. This day, — this day of the coming of
the Son of man, has another dawn than that which

---

[1] " We may be wont to divide the advent for mercy from the advent for judgment, by an intervening tract of ages. In the prophets
they are brought together. The apostle refers to Jesus the words
of the prophet whom the Church has called the Prophet of the Advent, *a bruised reed shall he not break, till he send forth judgment unto
victory, and in his name shall the Gentiles trust.*" (Maurice, *Sermons*,
vol. iii. p. 2.)

breaks in the eastern sky, and another close than that which belongs to the hours marked by the swing of the pendulum. For men and nations there are courses which have no measure in the finite: they have an infinite import and reality. There are paths of spiritual death and life, *the righteous enter into eternal life, and the wicked into eternal punishment.*

This judgment is not formed simply in the distribution and transmission of *things that are seen.* It does not find the issues of the actions of men only within the limits of a physical process, and as affecting a life concluded in that process, but it is a judgment which regards human action as having a spiritual character, and therefore an eternal significance.

This judgment is not, therefore, subject to finite limitations. It is not the exclusive incident of a certain time and a certain locality. The Christ says they that are in their graves shall come forth, — *they that have done good to the resurrection of life, and they that have done evil to the resurrection of judgment;* — and this is the evidence of the character and continuation of ethical conditions. This judgment is in the hour that cometh and now is, but it is not limited to the present, and it does not detach the future from the present. There is in evil always a foreboding of judgment to come; there is a doom which sin bears within itself; there is a *looking for of judgment.* This judgment, in the distinction and manifestation of righteousness and wickedness, is real and ethical and eternal.

This judgment has its precedent in and is involved with the revelation of God to the world. The Christ says, *this is the judgment, that light is come into the world, and men loved darkness rather than light, because their deeds were evil.*

This judgment of the world is constant; it is continuous. It may come as in other days, as the world fares on, as men are eating and drinking and planting and building, claiming dominion over this earth. It may come with the close of one age and the beginning of another age. It may be with the end of an old world and the beginning of a new world. The disciples ask the Christ when the end shall be, when shall come the end of that age, and the appearing of the Son of man. The Christ, in the description of this judgment, with words that are awful in their imagery and in the burden that they bear, says to them, *this generation shall not pass away, till all these things be fulfilled.* The words are not indeterminate, but, — as if they were difficult to apprehend, and their sense was to be perverted in some duplicity of thought, and the notions of men which prevailed were to be maintained as the substitute for them, — they are preceded by the most simple illustration drawn from nature, and they are followed by the most awful affirmation: *learn now a parable*

*of the fig tree: when his branch is yet tender, and
putteth forth leaves, ye know that summer is nigh;
so, likewise, when ye shall see all these things, know
that it is near, even at the doors. Verily, I say
unto you, this generation shall not pass, till all
these things be fulfilled. Heaven and earth shall
pass away, but my words shall not pass away.* It
was to come in a day and an hour that no man
knew. It was not merely an incident of time, but
its issues were eternal. It was to concern, not
only the exclusive nation, but all nations. It was
to come to that age and that generation, but it
might come in every age and to every generation.

It was a judgment by a person; it was not a
judgment subject to a formal law, with the adjudi-
cation of a tribunal of formal process. It was the
judgment of One who on this earth, and in the
changes of its history, had lived in the conflict
and the overcoming of evil and in the manifestation of the truth.

This judgment has a strict ethical import; it
has no other import. It is not on formal lines
which are the prescriptions of men, and from
which the condition of men and nations is determined. It allows no phrases current with religious
conventions; it is not a distinction of the religious
and the irreligious, with the various conceptions attached to these terms. It is a judgment in righteousness; *the righteous shall inherit eternal life, the
wicked shall go into eternal punishment.*

The law of the judgment of the world is that which is manifest in the coming of the Son of man. The law is in the coming of the Son of man, as it is for every generation in the trial and conflict of humanity. The Christ says, *I was an hungered, and ye gave me meat; I was thirsty, and ye gave me drink; I was a stranger, and ye took me in; I was sick, and ye visited me; I was in prison, and ye came unto me.* If the words call out surprise, and it may be suffer rejection as the law of the divine judgment, with the inquiry, *when saw we thee an hungered,* and *when saw we thee in prison?* the answer is, *inasmuch as ye have done it unto one of the least of these my brethren, ye have done it unto me.*

This judgment is universal. It is for every generation; there is no exemption. It is not the application of a law for which some substitute may be allowed. For those who have done good and faithful service, who have striven for righteousness, for the life of humanity, there is an entrance into the joy which was His in the sorrow and contradiction of earth, — the joy that transfigured the suffering and death of this earth, *Well done, good and faithful servant: enter thou into the joy of thy Lord.*

This judgment is universal, for it is in the coming of the Son of man. Its symbolism indicates the glory with which humanity is invested in the coming of the Son of man.

This judgment, in its ethical import, in its law of the oneness of the Christ with humanity, and in its realization in the life of humanity, is beyond the conceptions of the religious imagination. That has portrayed a judgment which is a remote and isolated scene. It is to be a high court where all are convened at its tribunal. There are scenic descriptions of this judgment, as in the writings of Josephus and through the wide ranges of oriental religious literature. It is remanded to a remote future. It is transposed beyond the confines of earth and the vulgar scenes which mark this bank and shoal of time. It is the precedent to an abode of happiness and an abode of misery, which are adjusted in contiguity to it. Then this life is defined as the emptiness, and the life beyond as the fullness of desire. Its law is only that of reversals and reprisals. It becomes, then, through the imagination, apprehended only as an event of strangeness, and is resolved into pictures and images. It is in its distant outline an object of vague and undefined dread. It is an event for which time may bring evasions. The removal of this judgment to a remote future, beyond them and their generation, heightens its appeal to the imagination, while it brings indifference to the conscience. It becomes a ground of apathy in the ethical life of men. But when this judgment is apprehended in its real and spiritual import, as near and at the very door, as the judgment of truth, then the conscience cannot be set at rest by any theories or dreams, nor by the undefined anticipations of evasion or delay.

The issues of this judgment have an eternal significance. The word æonian may denote an indefinite term of finite duration. But it does not assume that the judgment of this world is simply in finite terms, or that man is thus regarded simply as existing in finite relations. It has another quality; it has an infinite significance; it is not measured in material proportions. The consequence of righteousness and of every righteous action is in eternal life; and the consequence of wickedness and of every wicked action is in eternal death. Thus there is never in the conflict of an ethical life exemption from the consequences of evil. That these issues are not detached from the actual condition of man, and that they are not transferred to some remote date, has its evidence in the conscience and the consciousness of men.

In the ancient symbol it is written of the sequences of sin, *In the day that thou eatest thereof, thou shalt surely die.* S. Paul says, the law of death *has passed upon all men;* and again, *the wages of sin is death.* The Christ says, *he that believeth in me, though he were dead, yet shall he live: and whosoever liveth and believeth in me shall never die.*

There is thus a deeper significance than is measured in the abstract definitions of a formal logic,

in the words: *the things which are seen are temporal; but the things which are not seen are eternal.* S. Paul nowhere says the things which are
present are temporal, and the things which are
future are eternal. This notion does not consist
with his words, nor with the necessary conclusions
of thought. Its postulate is in the assumption of
the antithesis of the human and the divine; that
the human is lower and the divine upper; that
the temporal is present and the eternal is future;
that the finite is here and the infinite is there. It
does correspond with the prevalent notions of religious schemes. It becomes the ground of their
detraction of the life of humanity. It accords also
with that exclusive temper to which the religious
mind tenaciously clings in its apprehension of the
future, and which, as a religious sect, it holds
strongly in the measure of its sectarianism. It
consists further with indifference to the ethical
life, the life of righteousness, and it brings a rid-
dance to the conscience of men and nations of the
sequences of their unrighteousness, and of their
breaking of the commandments of God, whose fulfillment is the life of humanity, by the transposition of these consequences to a remote future. It
brings an illusive security, when the punishment
of wickedness and the recompense of righteousness
should have a stronger assertion. That the words
themselves at last become emptied of all meaning
by the religious schools and by the physical schools

furnishes only another illustration of that law of the spiritual and divine ethic: *from him that hath not, shall be taken away even that which he hath.* The Christ answers his disciples: *The disciples came and said unto him, Why speakest thou unto them in parables? He answered and said unto them, Because it is given unto you to know the mysteries of the kingdom of heaven, but to them it is not given. For whosoever hath to him shall be given, and he shall have more abundantly; but whosoever hath not, from him shall be taken away even that he hath. Therefore speak I to them in parables; because they seeing see not; and hearing they hear not, neither do they understand. And in them is fulfilled the prophecy of Esaias which saith, By hearing ye shall hear and shall not understand; and seeing ye shall see and shall not perceive: for this people's heart is waxed gross, and their ears are dull of hearing, and their eyes they have closed; lest at any time they should see with their eyes, and hear with their ears, and should understand with their hearts, and should be converted, and I should heal them; but blessed are your eyes, for they see, and your ears, for they hear. For verily I say unto you, that many prophets and righteous men have desired to see those things which ye see, and have not seen them, and to hear those things which ye hear, and have not heard them.*

The eternal is the name of God; its meaning is

more than with no beginning and no ending.   The
name of God is not thus summed up in negations;
these do not constitute his eternity.   S. John
says, *this is eternal life, to know thee, the only
true God, and Jesus Christ, whom thou hast sent.*
It is a spiritual life, a life not dependent on nor
determined by things visible, but in relation with
the Father and the Son, in fellowship with the
Holy Spirit.

The separation from the light and the knowledge of God, the rejection of all relation to him
and to humanity in him, involves eternal death.
But in this separation man is not left in abandon-
ment; the wrath of God follows and abides on any
man who continues in sin, not on man as in a condition of necessity, where a dualistic development
is realized and no unity can be attained, and
where his doom is irrevocable, that no redemptive
power or grace can abate it, but the wrath of God
continues and abides on man because he is related to God.   It were woe for man, if, left with
sin, no judgment followed him.

The consequence of wickedness is eternal punishment, and this is the assertion of an immutable
principle.   The punishment is eternal.   But to
identify this with an irrevocable doom is to set a
finite limit to the divine redemption and to its perfect realization.   It brings a section of the human
race into an ultimate condition of fate, and not of
freedom.   The spiritual law is eternal, but not the

necessary continuance in sin of one child of earth and time.

The words in which the Christ says to his disciples that this judgment shall be pronounced, in the coming of the Son of man, — *Come, ye blessed of my Father, inherit the kingdom prepared for you from the foundation of the world,* — are divested of their meaning when they are separated from the words which complete them, which assert the law of this judgment in the oneness of the Christ with humanity. And the words, *Depart from me, ye cursed, into eternal fire, prepared for the devil and his angels,* when they are severed from this law, and are pronounced as the realization of a final dualism and an utter fatalism, with their transposition into the far hereafter, are dismissed, as there is no response in the life of humanity. The words, then, which should express the awful condemnation of sin and of every sin became weak and broken, and the whole subject is set aside as inconsistent with the relations of humanity, instead of bringing out the very ground of these relations.

It is said that if this eternal death, which is the sequence of sin, has a terminus, then eternal life may have. But while this holds these terms in finite measures, and thus empties them of their real meaning, it may be said that eternal death, the death of sin, the law which has passed upon all, has a terminus in the kingdom of the Re-

11

deemer.   And eternal life would have an end if it did not rest, if life and peace did not rest, in the will of God and the communion of the Spirit.

This eternal punishment is the manifestation of sin, for sin has in it the severance of all those relations to God and to man which are eternal in their foundation.   If man did not live in infinite relations there would be no condition of sin.

The sin is here, and the death of sin; the eternal punishment is here, and continues with the continuing of sin, and is the actual manifestation of the nature of sin.

There is in and from God infinite love for man, and infinite hatred for sin, and this infinite hatred for sin is the reflex of perfect love.   Sin is in itself destructive of love; as love is involved in the relations of men, and love has in itself an ethical quality that involves the hatred of sin.   Sin is in itself destructive of life; there is in it no element of unity; it is subversive of personality.   S. John says, *He that believeth hath eternal life; this is eternal life, to believe in God.*   The apostle says, *the life that I live is by faith in the Son of God.* It is not a life determined and concluded by physical limitations and conditions; it is above the limitations of the finite.

In its nature, sin, and every act of sin, has its sequence in eternal death; and every act unto righteousness, in the relation of humanity to the Christ and through him unto God, has its fulfill ment in eternal life. This is invariable; it is a principle not restricted to other ages and æons, to be made manifest only in other worlds. It is fulfilled now in the Christ, in his kingdom, in the coming of the kingdom of heaven on earth.

S. John says, *now are we passed from death unto life*. This is now. It is not away from the here and into the hereafter; it is not defined by the passage of boundaries, as in spatial relations, and by intervals of transition, as in temporal relations. But in a figurative way it becomes true, to use the phrase of Erskine, that man may be in one place in eternal life, and a rod beyond in eternal death; or in one hour in eternal life, and in another hour in eternal death. This eternal life and eternal death, these infinite relations, have become the conditions of the existence of man.

This eternal life is a life which death does not touch; for even death itself, which marks most clearly the sorrows of this finite world, is taken up and changed. It is a life which is eternal with God. The Christ says, *he that believeth in me, though he were dead, yet shall he live; and whosoever liveth and believeth in me shall never die.* The assertion of the issue of righteousness in eternal life, and wickedness in eternal punishment, is the assertion of a principle involved in the ethical relations of life, and it is consistent with the sequence of the redemptive life of the Christ in the world, because the ethical life of man has not its limitations within the finite. The end of righteousness is in eternal life, in the redemptive kingdom, in the coming of the Kingdom of Heaven.

CHAPTER VII.

THE life which is manifested in the coming of the Son of God, and has its realization in the eternal life of man, has also its verification in the coming of the kingdom of heaven.

The representation of heaven was an unreality, while still it was invested with the attractions of that which the eye had seen and the ear had heard, and it had entered into the heart of man to conceive.

The words which the Christ repeats are *the kingdom of heaven,* or *the kingdom of God.* The gospel is called *the gospel of the kingdom,* or *the gospel of the kingdom of heaven.*

This expression is drawn from the common political life of men, and refers to historical forces in the growth of society. It does not imply that a special sacredness attaches to this form, and this form has not the relative value which belongs in the traditions of the Hebrew and Greek and Roman life to the republic, but it is simply the common and contemporary form.

It is represented as a kingdom, and has its implication in the historical life of the world, but it is not measured by any temporal and spatial conditions in an external order; *it cometh not with observation.* It is not the product of historical forces, as these forces are limited and defined by strictly physical conditions. It is not derived from them. The Christ says, *My kingdom is not of this world.* It has a reality which does not attach to that which has its derivation and termination in the transient forms of the physical process of the world. It is real; it is not to succeed an actual, with an empty and abstract ideal, but in it is the realization of the ideal. It is not the vague field of visionary thought. It is not remote, that it should become inaccessible; it is open, and it is separated from earth by no external limitations, that it should be approached over measures of distance or tracts of time.[1]

It is not always before us, as if located in the hereafter, and ever on and away, and never to be gained. These are strong words, that stir the heart with their assurance, *the kingdom of heaven suffereth violence, and the violent take it by force.*

This coming of the kingdom of heaven is represented in the same words that describe the coming

---

[1] " *Eye hath not seen, nor ear heard, neither have entered into the heart of man, the things which God hath prepared for them that love him; but God hath revealed them unto us by his Spirit.* The world of which the apostle speaks is not a future, but a present revelation. This verse is often quoted, as if the apostle, by the things prepared, meant the glories of a world to be visible hereafter." (Robertson *Sermons*, vol. i. p. 25.)

of the Son of man on the earth. The Christ said, *Verily, I say unto you, that there be some of them that stand here which shall not taste of death, till they have seen the kingdom of God come with power.*

This kingdom, of which the annunciation was *the gospel of the kingdom of heaven*, had its realization in the coming of the Christ in the life of the Spirit. It came with the power of the Spirit, that no forces of this earth could overcome. The Christ says to his disciples, *Verily, verily, I say unto you, that ye shall weep and lament, but the world shall rejoice: and ye shall be sorrowful, but your sorrow shall be turned into joy. A woman when she is in travail hath sorrow because her hour is come; but as soon as she is delivered of the child, she remembereth no more the anguish, for joy that a man is born into the world. And ye now therefore have sorrow, but I will see you again, and your heart shall rejoice, and your joy no man taketh from you.* The perfected man of God was to come, as one who opens the perfect kingdom of God.

This end, however imperfectly construed in human society, was the aim of the endeavor of religion and the speculation of philosophy. In the latter form, in the construction of philosophy, it was, however imperfectly conceived, the object of the republic of Plato and of the city of Aristotle.

The illustrations of this kingdom are not those

of an abstract character, nor an appeal to the abstract imagination. It is ethical; it has no other description; it is *the kingdom of righteousness and peace and joy in the Holy Ghost.*

This kingdom has come, and it may be always coming; it is in the realization of righteousness in the life of humanity. It has come, and it is therefore no vacant dream; it is always coming, and it is therefore to be striven for with the energy and the endeavor of men.

The signs of the coming of this kingdom are not those that are to be written upon some distant skies that sweep around the earth they never meet. They are not the suggestions of the religious imagination. They are in the restored life of humanity; *the blind see, and the lame walk, and the poor have the gospel preached to them.* These are the signs of the coming of the kingdom of heaven that the evangelists record.

It is a kingdom that asserts and recognizes the presence of spiritual forces; it is of and over the spirits of men. It is in its ethical character to invest the work and duties of men, in the courses of time, with its own substantive strength. This is the ground of the words of S. Paul, *for your citizenship is in heaven.*

The relation of this kingdom to the common life of humanity is set forth in words which have no parallel: *Suffer little children to come unto me, and forbid them not, for of such is the kingdom of heaven.* These are words in which science, with the limitations of physical conditions, can find no significance. They consist with the assumptions of no religion, but they are justified to the world, and they are words which humanity shall keep in its heart, until the travail of time is over.

It has been noted that the pagan religious conceptions of heaven still prevail, and the thought and emotion of men are moulded by them. They determine the conception of this revelation, instead of being determined by it. The heavens are still far above us, above this spot which men call earth, and are carried on and away before us; they are still an elysian view; the happy fields are located in the future, and the religious imagination invests them with images of delight; they are held as some enchantment, to body forth some ecstatic dream. The pagan religious conception sets off this world by a separate boundary from the further confines of heaven and hell. The infinite spiritual depths and heights are not real for humanity. It is not with great, nor even with true, prelusive strains, but on vacant keys and with unanswering tones, as the philosophy of agnosticism would taunt us, that it utters its *De Profundis* and its *In Excelsis.* This pagan conception avoids the words of the Christ, *Behold the kingdom of God is within you.* It says that it is not within you. It says that here all still is nothingness, and all within is emptiness, though the Christ has come and the Spirit has

been given unto men ; and it describes this kingdom as inaccessible, and as always away and beyond.   It brings repose to the conscience and confines for the consciousness of men, while it leads
the imagination on with the representation of its
pictorial splendors.

The Christ uses the word heaven, but it is not
the repetition nor the fulfillment of the dream of
the pagan religions.   It . is not a transportation
nor an emigration from all the relations of humanity.   It is in the most critical passage, which is
the answer to the hope of the world, the expression of the perfect ethic, that the Christ says, *The
kingdom of God is within you.*

The words of the Christ are the gospel of the
kingdom.   The kingdoms of this world become
the kingdom of the Christ.   The old is passing
away, but it is not as if lost in some abysm of time,
*there shall be new heavens and a new earth, where-
in dwelleth righteousness.*

But the tribes of men succeed each other, and
the generations go, and the world seems to grow
very old, old beyond all the records upon its scarped
cliffs and worn shores.   We trace often some glory
in the past that does not seem to return.   It is
no satisfaction to know that it has, in the attrition
of chemical forces, been resolved into the elements.
There comes to us the sense of a glory that has
waned and gone.   And again, the signs of prog

ress seem often obscured, and the very texture of history woven and imbued with the follies and crimes of men. There seems often the evidence only of an aimless struggle and strife, with no other significance than the struggle and the strife, and that all at last is remerged into the physical elements.

We see not yet the glory that shall be. The indications of the fulfillment of that which kings and prophets sought seem very far off. We are subject to death, and we see not yet, in the life of humanity, the perfect conquest of death: *the last enemy that shall be destroyed is death.*

But not alone, in solitary visions, as to the protomartyr, when in the hour of death surrounded by fierce and cruel faces, the heavens are opened, to behold *the Son of man sitting at the right hand of the power of God.* The Christ, in his own perfect and perfected life, overcame death, and has opened the perfected kingdom of God. In his oneness with humanity is the ground of the hope of humanity. We see not now the glory of humanity through the conquest of death, but Jesus has that glory: *One in a certain place testified, saying, What is man that thou art mindful of him? Thou madest him a little lower than the angels; thou crownedst him with glory and honor, and didst set him over the works of thy hands; thou hast put all things in subjection under his feet: but now we see not yet all things put un-*

der him ; but we see Jesus, who was made a little lower than the angels, for the suffering of death, crowned with glory and honor, that he, by the grace of God, should taste death for every man.

The kingdom of heaven has come, it is coming, it is to come. It moves beyond the past and through the present, and the future rises beyond the present. The Christ said, *among them that are born of woman, there hath not risen a greater than John the Baptist; but he that is least in the kingdom of heaven is greater than he.*

There is a glory that is revealed, and a greater glory that is yet to be revealed. It leads us forth and forward, and while the life of man is in no continuing city, and is among things which do not abide, it may be with faith and hope and love. Thus faith and hope and love abide, and they bear him on, and even when they seem strange in this physical order, they are justified.

CHAPTER VIII.

THE condition in which a child is born, in the relation of the family and the nation, however rude and imperfect these relations may be in their development, in the ethical process of the world, calls out some elements of faith.

The faith which is the gift and the evocation of this revelation is involved with the conscience and the consciousness of men. It has in its source and process and end an ethical quality.

This faith has not its ground and end in an abstraction, as a law or a system. It is not a faith in a proposition or in a series of propositions, and it has not the necessarily external character that belongs to them. It is faith in a person, a righteous person, in whom there is the foundation, and through whom there is the realization of the life of humanity. It is faith in one who was before the world was, and has come into the world in the fulfillment of righteousness, for the redemption of the world. This faith is not an effort of man which is to be received at a relative value, as a substitute for another effort of man. It is not to be apprehended as in itself without an ethical quality, nor yet to be placed at a higher value than the ethical process of life. It is not isolated, but is related to hope and love, and each can but imperfectly exist without the other.

These have each no merely finite ground and end, as they rest in one who, being one with God, became one with man, and whose life was the fulfillment of righteousness in the life of the world.

This faith is in a righteous person, in whom is revealed the ground of the life of humanity, and through him and with him there is righteousness of life. This is an actual righteousness, and through faith righteousness is wrought and has its realization in life.

This is the significance of the justification of men by faith. It is not a formal act.[1] It is not simply an act of reputation. We are not reputed to be just through a formal relation, but we are made just through an actual relation. It is not forensic. In its forensic use this word denotes an acquittal of a charge, and not a remission of a penalty. It is not the authentication of a

---

[1] " The passion of Christ was not to be the substitute for our personal obedience, but the source of it. To justify is to make, not simply to account, men just." (Oxenham, *The Catholic Doctrine of the Atonement*, p. 86.) " This is not a fictitious righteousness, for then it would be a fictitious blessedness, but it is a real conformity to the will of God. *In thy seed shall all the kindreds of the earth be blessed. God, having raised up his son Jesus, sent him unto you first to bless you, in turning away every one of you from his iniquities.*" (Erskine, *Memoirs*, p. 187.)

justification in an external way; it is not a certification of character in an abstract way, with ethical indifferences. It is not the apprehension of this proposition by faith. It is, — righteousness through faith.[1]

It is of free grace, and of grace unto grace, as it is given to all, and through faith man is brought into an immediate relation with the Christ. It

[1] " The root of Luther's contention against the ancient theology lay rather in his substitution of faith in the sense of *fiducia*, or the laying hold of the merits of Christ by an act of trust, for the *fides formata*, or faith working by love, to which alone the catholic doctrine ascribes a justifying power." (Oxenham, *On the Atonement*, p. 31.) But the strength of the thought of Luther was in his recognition of faith, as immediate, in the relation of man with God, in the relation in Christ; so that it was not, as in external relations, that any power on earth, or priest or book, should stand between man and God. There was a profounder conception in the doctrine of Luther and Calvin, which gave it its strength in working toward the freedom of men and of nations. Its defect was, when it did not pass beyond a mere particularism or individualism, nor apprehend its relation to sacrifice, and came at last to be regarded as an intellectual apprehension, the conscious act of a mature intelligence, — the apprehension of a system, and the acceptance of this system became the standard of the faith.

" To merge justification in sacrifice, is the error of the Romanist; to merge sacrifice in justification, is the error of the Protestant." (Maurice, *Sermons*, vol. iv. p. 19.) This may indicate, and yet only in one way, their respective defects. The former failed to apprehend the immediate relation of man to God, of which it was the witness; and the latter came to apprehend faith as only the conscious act of the deliberate mind, which had not its ground in a sacrifice that was for the sin of the world. Thus it came to be a practical faith in a proposition or system, the act of a fiduciary, the engagement of a constabulary, and the work of its minister was that of one who holds the gospel, as if it had passed under his clientage, and its truths were to be distributed at his discretion.

has not its ground in the imputation of an external righteousness, and it has not, therefore, as its condition, faith in a system or service. It is the actual implanting of righteousness through relation with him, who has taken our nature, and in whom was the fulfillment of righteousness.

Through faith in a righteous person who, being one with God, became one with man, in the manifestation of perfect righteousness, man is brought into the righteousness of Christ. It is the way toward communion with the Christ.

Faith in its influence is retrospective, but more strictly, in its relation to Him who was and is and is to come, the words retrospective and prospective do not apply. It is faith in another; it loses its life in Him, to find its perfect realization of life. It is being in another, in a righteous person, and it has reference to the poverty of self alone with self, and to the destitution and disgrace and guilt of sin, that when one flees to Him, as to a refuge, guilt cannot hold him, shame cannot appall him, the universe cannot stay him; he is clothed with the righteousness and the freedom of God. There are no words strong enough to portray this life. The stains of guilt are all effaced. They are cleansed in the fountain of an undying love. The robes of earth are washed in the blood of the Lamb that was slain for the world. The costumes of selfishness and vanity are thrown away. The reproach of the world becomes lost in the distance, to be heard no more. There are no finite limitations for the spirit. It repeats the rude heroic strain, —

" Freely justified, I
Shall mount to the sky,
With the sun and moon under my feet."

Faith in a righteous person, in the Christ, who is the source of the life of the family and the nation, leads the individual away from himself, and in being for another he finds his real life, and enters into and partakes of a righteousness that is not a mere self-righteousness ; — a righteousness that he may resist, and the end is death, or that he may enter into, and may find his own life. It is this that has been wrought into the unity and strength and freedom of nations.

And this faith does not stay by itself. It goes out toward another, as it is faith in one who has given himself for another. It can exclude none. It becomes the ground of sacrifice. It blends with love. A man does not, then, rest on the quality or the relative excellence of his own faith, and that, as the act of the finite mind, can soon be determined in finite measures ; but faith itself rests on a righteous person, — one who, being one with God, has become one with man, in the realization of the perfect righteousness.

Faith works with hope and love ; it is *faith that worketh by love.* The controversy of faith and works has its ground in empty and abstract theo-

12

ries. True faith is one with works, and good works are one with faith, because both alike have righteousness for their end.

Therefore faith in the Christ brings us into that righteousness, in the fulfillment of which he came into the world. There is no legal fiction. There is no fictitious transference of righteousness, but there is an actual participation in the righteousness of life which had in the Christ its perfect fulfillment.[1]

Through faith there is communion with the Christ in his eternal life. S. Paul says, *he was raised again for our justification.* This righteousness that was vindicated over death, and declared in his resurrection from the dead, is ours, — the proper righteousness of man, and in him given to men.

The perfect manifestation of God is in the Christ. Through faith in the Christ there is for man the knowledge of the love of God. It is a faith in a force of life and love and light that is

---

[1] " *Looking unto Jesus, who is the author and the finisher of our faith.* The Epistle bids us look from our faith to a Living Person who is the only root of it, the only end of it. Our faith is not in itself, but in him; if we think of it, instead of him, it perishes." (Maurice, *Sermons*, vol. i. p. 79.)

Faith is not the condition of the love of God, but through faith there is the apprehension of the love of God, and doubt is removed and fear, in the knowledge and love of God. Mr. Erskine says, "The proclamation of forgiveness through the Christ alone will bring peace to those under condemnation. If it be assumed that forgiveness is not actual for any until he believes it, the attention is turned to the quality of his faith." (Erskine, *Memoirs*, p. 86.)

deeper than the forces of evil. S. John says, *Jesus cried and said, He that believeth on me believeth not on me, but on him that sent me.*

The love and the forgiveness of God, the will of God toward man, is made known to man in the Christ.

This love is the ground, and not the sequence, of faith. The Christ is *the author and the finisher of our faith.*

Through faith there is the knowledge of the love and the forgiveness of God, and through faith there is righteousness of life. There is, then, *no condemnation to him that believeth, who walks not after the flesh, but after the spirit.*

Through faith man comes into the life of God, the life of love and righteousness. This is the true life of man. It apprehends in the ground of life the love of God, and in the fulfillment of righteousness the will of God. This is the foundation of the life of the family and the nation and, though it may not seem justified in the physical process, without it —

> " The pillared firmament is rottenness,
> And earth's base built on stubble."

CHAPTER IX.

THE world is redeemed. This redemption is real, and it has in the life of humanity its realization. The world is redeemed in the Christ, and the process of history is in the realization of the redemption of the Christ.

The Christ redeemed the world by becoming himself the perfect redeemer. In his own life there was the attainment and the fulfillment of the perfect righteousness. It was a life in the world of the manifestation of perfect truth to self in the life of the Spirit.

The Christ redeemed the world by becoming one with humanity, in the life of the world. The Christ became man. The life of humanity is in its realization, in righteousness and freedom, one with the life of the Christ. The redemption that he has wrought is the redemption of humanity. It is for us men.

The Christ redeemed the world by the manifestation in it of a life consistent with the knowledge of the source and the destination of life. There is, therefore, no power to come forth out from the beginning or the end, from the first to the last, with intimations of force or fear, that can claim subjection from man, or assert dominion over him, or can effect the subversion of the love that is at the source and centre of all things, or the disruption of the unity that is in the will of God, that is manifesting itself in the reconciliation of all things. The Christ says, *I know whence I came, and whither I go;* and again, *I am the first and the last, the beginning and the end; I am he that was and is and is to come.*

The Christ redeemed the world by the manifestation and realization in the life of humanity of the coming and life of the Spirit. It is redeemed by the power of the Spirit. The life of man is lifted above physical limitations, and is not determined and concluded in the process of physical forces and forms. It is not merely a projection of an animal existence, subjected to fleshly impulses and the satisfaction of fleshly appetites. It is not a life determined by external relations or external circumstances. It is the life which is not mortal. It has the strength and freedom of the Spirit.

The Christ redeemed the world by the realization of a perfect life, in the fulfillment of perfect righteousness, in oneness with humanity, and in the conflict with and the conquest of all the forces, by which humanity is alienated from God, and men are alienated from each other. It was the conquest of all the forces by which humanity is enslaved and tortured and divided and destroyed. He met the forces of the world and their temptations. The display of their rewards for subordination to the pursuit of selfish ends was brought before him, but he did not yield to them. The trial of the world was open to him, but he was not changed nor swerved by it, that his life should be shaped by the world. The Christ passed through death, but he overcame death. It was the conquest of life over death. The words of the Christ are, *I have overcome the world,* and again he says, *to him that overcometh will I grant to sit with me in my throne, even as I also overcame, and am set down with my Father in his throne.*[1]

[1] There are two representations of the work and sacrifice of the Christ in controversy with the position in this chapter. The one regards the atonement as a *legend*, although one of the most beautiful of the legends of the world. The Father sends the Son; the Son offers the sacrifice required, and returns to the Father. It has the unity and action of a drama. The myths gather around some legendary hero. It is beautiful as a drama, but far away from the world, to form only a mythology for the poet and superstitions for the people.

The other regards it as a *scheme of divinity.* Justice demands satisfaction. Its penalties must be executed with indifference as to the innocent or the guilty, if only the law be maintained. Mercy contends with justice, and wrath is averted when justice is appeased by this actual substitution, and this legal fiction. On this system faith rests, and the only security from these penalties is through its adoption.

These views are not far apart; they are abstractions; the one, in a formal way, is mythological, the other logical, but beginning and ending in mere formulas. They are throughout in controversy with the position here given. There is in the redemption the manifestation of God, the revelation of that which is eternal in the being of God, and through it man is raised to an eternal life with God.

The redemption of the world in and through the Christ was the manifestation of the will of God. The suffering and death of the Christ did not change the will of God. It was in the fulfillment of the will of God. The Christ says, *Lo, I come to do thy will;* and again, *I have declared thy name unto them and will declare it.*[1] The expression of the completeness of his redemptive work is in the words, *I have glorified thee on the*

[1] The catechism of Trent, explaining the reasons why the Son of God suffered, says one cause consisted, "in the crimes and vices which men have perpetrated from the beginning of the world till now, and shall perpetrate henceforth to the end of time; for in his death the Son of God contemplated the atonement and obliteration of the sins of all ages." (*Cat. ad Paroch.*, Pars I. c. v.)

"The death of the Christ was the perfect manifestation and the consummation of his faith in the Father." (Campbell, *On the Atonement*, p. 258.)

"Prophets and just men, under the old law, did and suffered much to bear testimony to the truth; but their obedience, like their testimony, was imperfect. He alone could make a perfect oblation of the human will; he alone as man could make an act of perfect contrition, who knew as God the fullness of the eternal love, and saw as God sees it the reality of the contradiction to that love." (Oxenham, *On the Atonement*, p. 77.)

"The perfect obedience of the Son discovers the perfect loving will of the Father. Infinite forgiveness and charity are shown to be at the root of all things; forgiveness and charity that are only seen, only satisfied, only made effectual by submission and sacrifice; forgiveness and charity that are not intended only to flow forth upon men, but to flow into them, to become a part of their character and being." (Maurice, *Sermons*, vol. iii. p. 380.)

S. Leo says of the relation of the Father and the Son, "One is the kindness of their mercy, as the sentence of their justice, nor is there any division of action where there is no diversity of will." (S. Leo, *Serm.* xxii. 4.)

earth : I have finished the work which thou gavest me to do.

The redemption of the Christ was the manifestation of ·the love of God for the world. It is thus that in the incarnation, the atonement has its beginning, and the one is involved in the other. It manifests the love of God. It was not the ground of that love, and it was not the condition which only in a provisional form justified that love, but the love of God for the world was the motive which went toward the redemption of the world : *God so loved the world, that he gave his only begotten Son :* S. John says, *herein is love, not that we loved God, but that he loved us, and sent his Son to be the propitiation for our sins.* *We love him because he first loved us.* There can be here no measure of the infinite love, —

> " Mine was the life that was won,
> And thine was the life that was given."

The redemption of the Christ was the manifestation of that which is eternal in the being of God. It was not simply a provisional work, which had its ground in a preceding circumstance. It had not its origin in a transient condition, and it was not simply an adjustment to an antecedent condition. It was *the Lamb slain from the foundation of the world.*

The redemption of the Christ has then no finite limitations. It has no measures of time. It is not limited by our computations of the years on this earth : *the Christ, a minister of the sanctuary and of the true tabernacle which the Lord pitched, and not man, entered in once into the holy place, having obtained eternal redemption for us.*

The redemption of the Christ is wrought in his oneness with humanity, in and through the life of humanity.[1] Through the relation of the Christ with humanity the redemption of the world has its continuous realization in the life of humanity. The law which was fulfilled in the Christ is the law of the life of humanity. The Christ says, *whosoever will come after me, let him deny himself, and take up his cross daily, and follow me.* Thus S. Paul writes of *the fellowship of his sufferings.* He speaks again of *filling up that which is behind of the afflictions of Christ.* He says, *I bear in my body the marks of the Lord Jesus.* This expression takes on the intensest form ; he says, *I am crucified with Christ.* He writes of his glory in the cross, wherein *the world is crucified unto me, and I unto the world.* He writes of *always bearing about in the body the*

---

[1] " One only who was God and man could bring man again into communion with God. But it is rather his assumption of our nature in all its fullness, than his death alone, that the Fathers dwelt upon. He is the representative man, the second Adam, the head of the body, who recapitulates in himself, as they are fond of expressing it, the whole human race, and imparts to them, through the union of their nature with his, a new principle of life, in whose death all die, in whose resurrection all are made alive. This is the great argument of Athanasius." (Oxenham, *On the Atonement,* p. 144.)

dying of the Lord Jesus, that the life also of Jesus may be manifested in our body. There is the same expression in the words of S. Peter, *ye are called, because Christ also suffered for us, leaving us an example, that we should follow his steps.* The suffering of humanity is transfigured. The suffering and sacrifice of the world is not henceforth merely in the projection of a physical process, nor with other alternatives of suffering and sacrifice in the development of a historical process; and thus the sacrifice of the soldier who dies in battle for the nation is not the mere conformance to a law of historical necessity, but in such suffering and sacrifice there is the redemptive life of the world.

We are called, since the Christ has given himself a sacrifice for us. In a correspondence with other types and forms of sacrifice, it is written, *wherefore Jesus also, that he might sanctify the people with his own blood, suffered without the gate.* This is made the ground of a principle of duty, and we are bidden, *let us go forth, therefore, unto him without the camp, bearing his reproach.* This is not the suffering of the Christ as an equivalent for the suffering of humanity, nor as a substitute for humanity; it is the sacrifice of the Christ fulfilled in humanity. It is the adoption of the sacrifice by participation by humanity; *let us go forth, therefore, unto him without the camp, bearing his reproach.* The Christ had said, *if any man will come after me, let him take up his cross and follow me;* and he said of his disciples, in their continuing relation with him, *Ye shall drink indeed of my cup, and be baptized with the baptism that I am baptized with.*

There is thenceforth in the life of humanity the manifestation of redemptive forces. There are redemptive forces continuing in the coming of the Christ and in the life of the Spirit, in his redemptive kingdom on the earth. They come forth in the life of righteousness in the family and the nation. These are the forces which work through the life of humanity, in conflict with the evil of the world. The law of sacrifice becomes, then, the law of life.[1] The contradiction in the revelation of the Christ is verified and solved in the course of history, and the words are justified: *he that loseth his life shall find it.* The work of sacrifice goes on in the process of history.

---

[1] The theories of life, in the physical school, cannot wholly efface the consciousness of this law of self-renunciation, though their assertion of it may be inconsequent. "There need be no disappointed ambition, if a man were to set before himself a true aim in life, and to work definitely for it; no envy, if he considered that it mattered not whether he did a certain great thing, or some one else, if only it were done; no grief from loss of fortune, if he estimated at its true value that which fortune can bring him, and that which fortune can never bring him; no wounded self-love, if he had learned well the eternal lesson of life,— self-renunciation." (Maudsley, *On Responsibility in Mental Disease*, p. 210.) This recognizes an element of self-renunciation, but it has no ground in a life determined in physical limitations; it has no justification in a life in finite conditions. It is only because it has another and higher ground that it becomes *the eternal lesson of life.*

The Lamb that was slain from the foundation of the world prefigures its course. The condition of the life of the last nation becomes the same as the first, the sacrifice of the worthier of her children. Their sacrifice is the perpetuation of the life of the nation; their sacrifice is the way to her deliverance from slavery; their sacrifice is the ground of her unity and peace. This was not the sacrifice of a certain number of men for a certain other number of men; it was not the sacrifice of a certain smaller number of men that a certain larger number might be exempt from sacrifice, and might live in self-indulgence. It was sacrifice for the life of the nation. It was life through death. It was that in all there might be the spirit and recognition of the law of sacrifice, the self-renunciation of the individual, which is the only way to the perfect self-realization, and the beginning of the life that is eternal. This law has a moral ground, which cannot be comprehended in the atomy of human society, nor in the severance through society of the superior from the inferior, nor in the apprehension of it as an accumulation of private interests, nor in any detachment of it from God.[1]

---

[1] " The atonement is the manifestation of the hope of God for man. The nature of that hope which was in God for man, and which the atonement has brought within the reach of our spirits, has indeed been necessarily determined by our primary and ultimate relation to God as the Father of our spirits." (Campbell, *On the Atonement*, p. 187.)

Henceforth the law of sacrifice becomes the law of power. In this world of forms the symbols of sacrifice become the symbols of power. The Lamb that was slain from the foundation of the world becomes, in the mystic vision of S. John the Divine, the Lamb that sits in the midst of the throne. This type is not lost in history. The manifestation of power is not in a separation from men, nor in the assertion of a dominion over men, but in the service of men. It is not the Cæsar that becomes the enduring power with men. The nation, which in this last age, is the exponent of the highest historical forces, has its foundations, its unity and order and freedom, laid in sacrifice. But it is through sacrifice, as through the negation of this finite world, that there is the coming of the life that is eternal, the realization of the life that is infinite.

The sacrifice of the Christ was the perfect and finished sacrifice, — the sacrifice of one who bore the burden of this finite world, in the fulfillment of the perfect righteousness, the manifestation of the perfect love, the revelation of the perfect life. It was the will of God before the foundation of the world; it was the sufficient sacrifice for the sin of the whole world, the foundation of eternal life and unity and peace.

The redemption through the Christ was wrought

in the satisfaction of love and justice, in the fulfillment of the will of God in the creation of the
world, — the foundation that was before and beneath the foundations of this finite world. It was
the satisfaction of God, the satisfaction of Christ
and of the conscience of men. And love is inexorable as justice, and involves duty as the sum of
the commandments of the law. It was not the
satisfaction of justice apart from love, nor as the
precedent condition of the revelation of love. For
in relation to the law there was not merely the
satisfaction, but the fulfillment of the law. It
was not a satisfaction of justice by the imposition
upon the innocent of the punishments of the
guilty, nor, by the substitution of an equivalent
of the same measure through a series of legal fic-
tions, and in that there would be no measure of
gain. In a higher sense justice is satisfied when
righteousness is actualized on the earth. Justice
is vindicated when it is asserted and established.
It is not a compensation to balance injustice that
is required, nor an equivalent for sin or for the
sequences of sin, but the power to overcome evil,
and to bring men out of sin.

The suffering and the death of Christ did not
take away the wrath of God against sin, for if
any man continue in sin *the wrath of God abideth
on him.* There was in the Christ the strongest
assertion of the wrath of God against sin. It was
the announcement of the woe that is to follow sin

in men and nations. But it were woe if the wrath of God was averted from sin. It were woe to men and nations if there were no judgment, in which the consequences of evil courses were manifested.

The Christ redeems the world from sin and from the sequences of sin. The Christ, coming into the world where sin was, endured in it the effects of sin. He endured death; *he was wounded for our transgressions, and bruised for our iniquities.*

The redemption of the world is from sin and unto righteousness. It is from the bondage of sin into the freedom of God. It is of the world unto God.[1]

This redemption of the spirit of man is from the forces by which, as external to itself, it is determined, and through this redemption from these forces its life becomes a self-determined life, in truth to self, the life of freedom. This freedom is not the detachment of self, but it is in the life of the spirit; it is not the isolation of self and its vacancy, but the energy and communion of the life of the spirit. It is the rescue from evil,

---

[1] " S. Paul says every sacrifice implies communion with the being to whom it is offered. So the end of Christ's incarnation and death was to establish a complete communion between men on earth and their Father in heaven, which may be most real now, but the full fruition of which can only be when all the evil which resists the divine righteousness and love is entirely vanquished." (Maurice, *Sermons,* vol. i. p. 43.)

as evil is alien to the spirit of man. It is the deliverance from the dominion of sin, from the principalities and powers which would claim to themselves the subjection of the spirit, and assume a domination over it, *for sin shall not have dominion over you.* This is the deepest expression of the experience of life : *if we be dead with Christ we believe that we shall also live with him : knowing that Christ, being raised from the dead, dieth no more ; death hath no more dominion over him; for in that he died he died unto sin once, but in that he liveth he liveth unto God.*

This redemption of the world is through the suffering and death and resurrection of the Christ. This sacrifice of the Christ was in his coming into the world; it was the earthly life of service; it was the last sacrifice in death. It was not simply the sacrifice of one for another; it was the sacrifice of him who had become one with humanity for the life of humanity. It was the sacrifice that was the fulfillment of love. This is not the negation of self with the implication of the cessation of self, an utter nihilism, but there is the perfect self-realization, the realization of life. It is not the dethronement, but it is the enthronement of life. It is not for life to be conquered by death; it is the conquest of death. It is a sacrifice of self, and this is its ethical significance, but in it is the attainment of life. The law of self-renunciation is the

law of self-realization, and the way through death
is unto life. And as death in the physical process involves always isolation and the severance of
the relations of life, so in the life of the spirit it
is a communion and an eternal life, since *the Christ
has partaken of death for every man.*[1] It is not,
therefore, the death of the Christ in itself that is
to be regarded primarily; it is the conquest of
death in the Christ.[2]

There was a significance in the judgment and
condemnation of the Christ, by the world, by ritual and imperial tribunals. He came to the death
of a slave on this earth. For the ignorance of
the multitude that made itself the instrument of
the world's derision and the world's torture he
offered the prayer of forgiveness to the Father;
*Father, forgive them, for they know not what they
do.* To them, to whom it seemed the profanation
of the universe, that the Christ the Son of God
was to become the Son of man he uttered the
transcendent words : *The high priest asked him
again, and said unto him, Art thou the Christ, the
Son of the Blessed ? And Jesus said, I am, and
ye shall see the Son of man sitting on the right
hand of power, and coming in the clouds of heaven.*

---

[1] " The atonement is truly apprehended only when the work of
Christ, through which we have the remission of sins that are past,
is contemplated in direct relation to the gift of eternal life." (Campbell, *On the Atonement*, p. 133.)

[2] " The death of the Christ is never to be considered apart from
the resurrection." (Rothe, *Dogmatik*, vol. ii. p. 220.)

The Christ met death in the last conflict. The Christ did not evade death, nor open a way to a continuous existence on the earth, in this domain of time and space, that was preëmpted from death. It was in order that by death *he might deliver them who through fear of death were all their lifetime subject to bondage.* S. Paul says, *in that he died he died unto sin once, but in that he liveth he liveth unto God.*

The Christ overcame death. It was the realization of a life that was for humanity above death.

There was in the death of the Christ the realization of the divine transfiguration, of which the witness had been given in the historical life of humanity, — which had its evidence *in the law and the prophets.* Then the sorrow of the world was turned into joy. Then the isolation and death of the world was transmuted into life, in the communion of God.

The redemption of the world is from sin. The Christ comes, — *the Saviour of the world.* In him is the revelation of the living truth; in him is the perfect righteousness. He is the only Saviour, as there is one truth alone and absolute, in which man may rest. There is one God, one humanity, one divine and perfect redeemer, though there be many through whom this redemption is wrought, that God may be all in all. It is said of him, *he shall save his people from their sins.* S. Paul says, *Christ gave himself for us that he might redeem us from all iniquity* : he is *the Lamb of God which taketh away the sin of the world.* This salvation is not an incident of the past, nor deferred to the future ; the apostle says, *now is the day of salvation.* This is the ground of the energy and freedom of the spirit, and its peace.[1]

There is the assurance that the redemption of the world shall have its perfect realization, *in Christ shall all be made alive.* This is not the assertion of a law of physical necessity, as the iteration of a fate, that forces of compulsion shall constrain the will. This redemption is to bring man out from the subjection to forces which are external to the will and are alien to the spirit of man, and into freedom. It is from the bondage and the doom of sin. It is with the salvation of man, that there comes alone a higher energy and ampler freedom. Through sin the slavery of man exists, and every sin brings a deeper bondage, and a consequent degradation, by a law of moral conditions ; but the forces of evil are met by redemptive forces, and in the fulfillment of the true and eternal being of man. These redemptive forces

---

[1] " Cast thy burdens upon the Lord. For he to whom past and present and future are all one, He who is and was and is to come invites you to claim fellowship with Him in his Son your Lord. Seeking him you do cast away those burdens which are pressing down your spirit, the burden which he bore, who bore the sins of the world. You can come with all your darkness into his light." (Maurice, *Sermons*, vol. i. p. 74.)

shall prevail, with the fulfillment of the life of humanity in God.

To the inquiry, *Are there few that be saved?* the answer is, *strive to enter in at the strait gate.* This energy that strives is the first element of freedom. It is the call to no apathy and vacancy of will; it overcomes the enervation of the spiritual powers of man which sin has wrought. It is the quickening of life. It affirms that *he that loveth is born of God,* and the end of the redemption is *the manifestation of the sons of God.* It asserts that he that *believeth shall be saved, and he that believeth not shall be condemned;* and it sets forth this condemnation, *that light has come into the world, and men loved darkness rather than light, because their deeds were evil;* and, therefore, *there is now no condemnation to them which are in Christ Jesus, who walk not after the flesh, but after the spirit.*

It does not assert in any moment, for any man, in the here or the hereafter, an irrevocable doom. Its end is to save man from sin and from the doom involved in sin. It does not place any without hope; it makes hope a virtue, difficult as all virtue is in this world, but still one with faith and love, and if illusive, then also faith and love, for which the same ground and end is revealed, are illusive. It asserts that men and nations may choose darkness, and refuse to recognize the redemption and revelation of the love of God, and to believe in it, and to work for the realization of righteousness and freedom in the life of humanity. It asserts the judgment that shall come, and bring the forces of evil that have their strength in darkness to the light.   In the oneness of the Christ with humanity, it asserts the blessing which shall be upon those who minister in the simplest offices, and to the lowliest, and the judgment on those whose action shall tend to the degradation of men and of nations.

There is in the Christ the redemption of the world, — it is *the redemption of the world.*   The evidence of love and freedom has its imperfect expression, in this physical world.   There is, indeed, in the forms of nature, that which may recall to man his origin and destiny, which she bears not in herself; and the lilies as they grow, and the sun that has shone, and the rain that has fallen upon the just and the unjust, may verify the thought of him who hath not left himself without a witness, — though it be only to him that receives it; and the clouds that gather in the evening sky may awaken the hope of another dawn; and nature, even from her embers, may bring the intimations of immortality with the remembrance of what seems so fugitive.   But it is in this revelation that there is manifest, through the negation, the fulfillment of the finite world.   In this revelation the knowledge of the final cause and end of the world is open to man.   In the reflected light that comes to the darkness and trial of earth, and reaches the depths of the variance and the sin and the suffering of the world, the end of the physical process is manifested, in the fulfillment of unity, and in the realization of perfect love and perfect freedom. It is the end of the struggle of human existence, it is the transfiguration of the sorrow of earth. It does not veil the pain of this physical world; it unveils its end, in the realization of the freedom and relationship of humanity with God. In words which preclude limitation, and embrace the entire physical process, S. Paul says, *the whole creation groaneth and travaileth together in pain, waiting for the manifestation of the sons of God.*

The Christ in the redemption of the world accomplished the reconciliation of the world unto God; *God was in Christ, reconciling the world unto himself.* It is the reconciliation of an existence, in which man is born into a condition in which sin and the effects of sin are transmitted, in its hereditaments, an estate of sin and misery, in which there is suffering and death. It is not the reconciliation of diametric forces which are opposites, and this would be the postulate and require the conclusions of a dualism; it is not the reconciliation of the holy and the profane, the wicked and the righteous, the forces which are of the world and the forces which are of God, — it is the reconciliation of the world unto God. The finite is transmuted into the infinite, the earthly is lifted unto the heavenly.[1]

The redemption of the world has its end in the realization of the freedom of humanity in God. The end of the world is the fulfillment of the life of humanity in God; God is free, and will have all men to be free, with the freedom of the sons of God. The apostle says, *the Christ came to redeem them that were under the law, that we might receive the adoption of sons.* He says, *Christ suffered for us, that he might bring us to God.* This freedom is real in the life of the spirit. This freedom is not a mere indifference, as is implied in the power of choice, although this power is incident to the development of freedom in this finite world. It is not a negative freedom, that is void of all moral

---

[1] The reconciliation of the world is perfect, and it is therefore that we are bidden to live *as sorrowful, yet always rejoicing.* It is beyond the thought merely of the restoration, and the Church repeats in its high service the words of S. Augustine, *O felix culpa, quae talem et tantum meruit habere Redemptorem.* " It destroys evil with good : the central principle of the atonement must be the same as the central principle of the whole revelation; Christ satisfies justice by establishing righteousness, not as in a drama, nor in any pictorial or representative way, but as a fact. What can condemn sin, but that which destroys sin; what vindicates justice but that which makes it a universal reality." (Munger, *A Statement of Theology,* p. 20.)

" God the Son came upon earth to satisfy his own justice as much as to satisfy his Father's, and for the accomplishment of his Father's love to man as much as for his own." (Benson, quoted in Oxenham, *In the Atonement,* p. 89.)

determination and energy. It is not a formal freedom, which is realized in the maintenance of external conditions. It is one with righteousness; it is not, then, a mere conformity to an external law. The redemption could not be, through the application of an external law. S. Paul says, *by the deeds of the law there shall no flesh be justified.* It could only be in the life of the spirit, in the righteousness and freedom of the spirit. This is not a conformance to an abstract law, and it is not a formal freedom. It is spiritual and real.[1] It is from the condition of a servant, into the relation of a son. It is from the bondage of sin into the freedom of God. It is only from the being of God, and the realization of freedom that we come to the knowledge of the infinite. And man only has a perfect freedom, as he rises into the life of

[1] This freedom does not belong to man, as his being is determined in the necessary relations of the physical process. It has not its measure in the physical process, —

> "Surelier it labors, if slowlier,
> Than the meters of star or of sun."

This freedom is gained in the overcoming of evil; it is the overcoming of evil with good.

"Many may rise up in judgment against those who live in other circumstances, to whom the name of Freedom has become so much a name of course, that they jest at it as a school-boy phrase, or ask how much they are richer for it, or wish they could barter it for some of the conveniences of despotism. This purposeless, heartless temper, as it increases, tends to the fulfillment of its own desires. Liberty cannot last when the aspiration for it has perished. Despotism is sure to come when it is beckoned for." (Maurice, *Sermons*, vol. iv. p. 91.)

God. There is alone no limitation there, and the personality of man, as it has its source in God, has its real life with God. There the self-renunciation and the obedience of the human will is fulfilled in the absolute will; and the bare resistant forces of the will are transmuted into consistent forces of life and its energy. It is in these relations that the human will attains its real freedom, but apart from them, and apart by itself, within the limitation of self, it is not free. In the physical process and in its conditions, man has no freedom, and it is attained only in the relation of man with God.

It has the energy of the Spirit, as spontaneity and originality are presumed in freedom and are implied and realized in personality. It is not summed up in negations: *In the last day, that great day of the feast, Jesus stood and cried, saying, If any man thirst, let him come unto me and drink. He that believeth in me, out of his belly shall flow rivers of living water. But this he spake of the Spirit, which they that believe on him should receive; for the Spirit was not as yet, because that Jesus was not yet glorified.*

The realization of the redemption of the Christ is in the eternal life. It is unto life; it is beyond the power of the transient; it is not apprehended in the ephemeral and the phenomenal; it is not fulfilled in relations that are simply spatial and temporal. It is necessary that he, through whom the redemption of man is accomplished, should be the perfect man, for that is the ideal of every man and of the spirit; and that he should be one who was, and who shall be when the heavens and earth are gone.

The death of the Christ has given to the common life of humanity an infinite consequence. It is death that is common to all men, and the Christ has partaken of death for every man. It is the perfect communion of God with man, through the suffering and death of this earth.

The redemption of the Christ was not formal. It was not a formal consistence with certain conditions of an abstract scheme, as in the fulfillment of a contract. It was not thus the conformance with a plan. It was not the work of one who came as the substitute for another, and whose righteousness was then made the subject of transfer to another, on conditions of faith, as in a certain stipulation.[1] It was not an act for the illustration of certain ethical requirements, and thus designed to secure certain impressions as an exhibition, an incident with certain spectacular

---

[1] " The doctrine of Scripture, so far from being the doctrine of mere substitution, is a protest against that doctrine; it makes accurate provision for moral claims; it enforces conditions on the subject of sacrifice; it attributes a rational ground of influence and mode of operation to the sacrifice." (Mozley, *University Sermons* p. 174.)

effects. It was a spectacle to men and angels, but of another and infinite reality.

The abstract schemes and systems of the atonement have their postulate in the notion that, while God apportions and must apportion to every instance and degree of transgression its proper punishment, it is not a subject of concern, whether the one who pays this be one who transgresses or another who is innocent, provided that the payment be an equivalent, and that he is under the necessity of cancelling the guilt, whenever the equivalent is tendered by any hand.[1] This assumes an analogy of a crime and a debt. It is not righteous.

The atonement was not provisional, as a subsequent arrangement to effect certain ends, in a situation in which certain defects had become apparent. It was not simply the adoption of a remedial system, in a condition in which sin and its sequences had appeared. It was that, for it was the coming of one who taketh away all our infirmities, and healeth all our sicknesses, but it was infinitely more ; it was the manifestation of that which was in the being of God, and its end was eternal life. It was the will of God, *before the foundation of the world.*

---

[1] "Judicial punishment can never be inflicted simply and solely as a means to promote a good other than itself, whether that good be the benefit of the criminal or of civil society; but it must at all times be inflicted on him, for no other reason than because he has acted criminally." (Kant, *Werke,* vol. ix. p. 180.)

It is not a transaction in the exchange of equivalents, in which certain advances are made, and certain results are secured ; and there is not, as in a rate of exchange, the substitution of one value for another value.   It is communion and not substitution, that is realized through death.[1]

It is not the taking away of the wrath of God against sin.   It is not the pacification of God, for it is the gift to man of the peace of God. It is the satisfaction of God in the creation of the world, for, through the divine redemption, the apostle writes of committing ourselves unto God *as unto a faithful Creator.*

---

[1] " *Who died for all, that they who live should not live unto themselves, but unto him.* We must believe that this love will mould society according to its law, nor suffer men to make another law for themselves, which is one of selfishness and hatred. In the faith that Christ's constraining love is the mightiest power in the universe, we must be, think, act. The same love must be acting more perfectly on those who have passed out of our world. Our relation to them does not rest on the strength of our affection or our memory. It is Christ's love, not ours, which binds them to us. In him they are dead, and in him only they have life." (Maurice, *Sermons,* vol. iii. p. 236.)

" Thou shalt purge me with hyssop, and I shall be clean; thou shalt wash me and I shall be whiter than snow, was the assurance of a man upon whose conscience lay the burden of adultery and murder. For these crimes, the sword was never to depart from his house. No petty penances, such as confessors lay upon kings, but such as God lays upon them and their subjects equally, the loss and rebellion of children, exile, sorrow without and within, were appointed for him. But he himself had a free spirit; he had dared to seek God's righteousness, to fly to him from his own evil, and therefore it had not power to hold him a prisoner." (Maurice, *Sermons,* vol. i. p. 93.)

It has not its ground in the faith of any man, and not thus by the faith of man is salvation, but its ground is in that love which faith can but imperfectly apprehend, and hope can but faintly forecast. It is still greater than faith can discern, and hope cannot discover its limit. S. Paul says, *God commendeth his love toward us, in that, while we were yet sinners, Christ died for us.* S. John says, *herein is love, not that we loved God, but that he loved us.*

In the course of the historical world, in the lives of men and of nations, there is suffering and sacrifice. It may be inferentially assumed that there is some law of suffering and sacrifice. It is not solely the impulse of nature, but as it prevails through the course of the physical world, it may be taken up and transmuted in the life of the spirit, and penetrated with an ethical aim. It has an ethical character, and there can be no ethical law in human life of greater significance. It is the evidence of the greater love in the relations of men, *greater love hath no man than this, that he lay down his life for his friend.* The phase of thought upon life, which describes it as the struggle for existence, recognizes this fact of suffering and in some form of sacrifice. But it is only in this divine sacrifice that these facts are justified. It is only in the suffering and sacrifice of the Christ that the suffering and sacrifice of the world has its true interpretation. It is only in this, that they are invested with a divine significance.[1]

There was in the atonement for the world the manifestation of God. It was the will of God in its fulfillment of righteousness. To him man may come, in the service that is perfect freedom, and in his election is peace in the knowledge and love of God, that the world cannot give, and cannot take away.

[1] " The moral teaching of Christ is the expression of the conscience of a people who had fought long and heroically for their national existence. In that terrible conflict they had learned the supreme and overwhelming importance of conduct, the weakness and uselessness of solitary and selfish efforts, the necessity for a man who would be a man, to lose his poor single personality in the being of a greater and nobler combatant — the nation." (Clifford, *Lectures and Essays*, vol. ii. p. 230.) These words are the expression of an imperishable truth, which the last age in the education of the world may learn as well as the first age in its historical courses. But because the nation has a divine and eternal foundation, it may learn, through sacrifice, the ground of its unity and peace. And the personality of man is not lost in it, but is lifted up and ennobled in it; for it has an immortal life; it has given to it the strength of an eternal victory. In the words of S. John the Divine, — and it is no mystic story for this generation, — its power is typified *in the throne of the Lamb*. But if the personality of man were to be lost and obliterated in its life, — in the coming of this greater and nobler combatant; if it were not here and in these relations, and through its own sacrifice to have its fulfillment ; — if it were not in losing its life to find it, then there could be no words of hope borne back to those involved in this evolution, and the memory of those who had offered themselves should be their mockery, as their names were repeated over the hollow earth they rounded with their graves.

It is the righteousness of God. The Son of God became the Son of man, and in his life is the fulfillment of righteousness. It is in the righteousness of the Christ, that humanity has its victory and its peace. Our love is weak and faltering, but in him is the eternal love. Our faith is dim and confused, but his faith is perfect. Our repentance is broken, and only imperfectly discerns the depths of variance and sin ; but his repentance is adequate, and his faith and his repentance are ours. We can only say as we come to him, in the communion with him which is his gift, *Thou only art holy ; thou only art the Lord ; thou only, O Christ, with the Holy Ghost, art most high in the glory of God the Father.*

CHAPTER X.

THE life, which the Christ has manifested to the world, becomes henceforth the life of the spirit.[1]

The Christ says, *it is expedient for you that I go away : for if I go not away the Comforter will not come unto you ; but if I depart I will send him unto you. When he, the Spirit of truth is come, he will guide you into all truth : for he shall not speak of himself; but whatsoever he shall hear that shall he speak. He shall glorify me : for he shall receive of mine and shall shew it unto you. All things that the Father hath are mine : therefore said I that he shall take of mine, and shall shew it unto you.* These words indicate a knowledge of a divine relationship, which is not a sequence of the experience of the world. They are the assertion of that which was to have its fulfillment henceforth in the life of humanity, the last, the greatest prophecy of humanity.

---

[1] The commemoration of the services of the Church on Christmas and Easter has come to have a common recognition, but the higher services are those of the Ascension Day and Whitsunday, the commemoration of the coming of the Spirit, and the conception which may be held of the former services is very deficient when they are separated from these which follow them.

Hence the judgment and the redemption of the world, and the life with God, are realized in and through the life of the spirit.

Hence the relation to the Christ is not an external relation, which is sustained in a formal historical circumstance, but it is a relation of and in the life of the spirit.

Hence the redemption of the world is not simply a deliverance from evil and its sequence, — a course of negations, but it is in the coming of the new life, which is the life of the spirit.

Hence the ethical life of man is in the life of the spirit, and this alone is the ground of a life which has elements that are substantial and eternal, in the truth and freedom which man has with God. The life of the spirit becomes the element of the life of righteousness and the life of freedom.[1] The righteousness is real which is a spiritual righteousness. It is not an external consistence with a formal command, as a prescript in the conduct of affairs; it is that, and further, it is a con-

---

[1] The demands of the masters in morals who represent its latest phases of thought, are very great; as Kant, who says, obey the command of reason within, — this you are bound to do; or Bentham, who says, do that which shall be for the greatest good of the greatest number. They lay heavy burdens upon the unequal shoulders of men. Mr. Clifford says, thou shalt not formulize. S. Paul says, *the law was a schoolmaster.* But it is only as man recognizes the Spirit given to each and to all men, the spirit of truth and love, it is only in the life of the spirit that these formulas become elements of strength; then they are not a weight to bear; they are highways for our advancement; they are the stones of the living temple.

formance that is in the life of the spirit. It is the fulfillment of the law, in the life and freedom of the spirit. It is not freedom from God, which has its assertion and realization in righteousness; it is the freedom of God. The words have increasingly their verification, *where the Spirit of the Lord is, there is liberty.*

Hence the life of man is brought into immediate relation, in its ground and continuance, with the life of God. It is not a relation through external conditions, to find its source and determination in them; it is in the life of the spirit.

Hence the relation to the Christ is realized in the life of the spirit. It is not a relation to Jesus of Nazareth, in the circumstantial condition which is comprised in certain contiguous relations. It may be a source of weakness, as the imagination occupies itself with this circumstance. The incident of this individual life is transient, as every incident of time, and subject to its conditions. The Christ says to those whom he sends forth to all nations: *in the name of the Father, and the Son, and the Holy Ghost, lo I am with you always, even unto the end of the world.*

The words of the Christ have not their ground in an external authority. The signature of their authority is not in the instrument in which they appear, but their verification is to the spirit. Their justification is to the conscience and the consciousness of men. It is, *verily, verily I say unto you.* The Christ says, *my words, they are spirit and they are life.* Thus the message that was given to the churches was always with a universal expression, *he that hath an ear let him hear what the Spirit saith unto the churches.*

The real life of humanity becomes henceforth the life of the spirit. The Christ says, *it is better for you that I go away ; the Spirit shall come, that will guide you into all truth.* There are in these days many voices with counsel for men ; — let us be satisfied with the limitations of a physical process which rejects all reference to another than a physical origin and end for the whole being of man, and accept only its course of necessity, and allow only the knowledge which is the result of the observation and investigation of physical organization and relations ; or come together and construct a new religion that may deepen and widen the religious life ; or acknowledge with reverence the unknown, with whatever predicates may be attached to it, to form from thence a religion ; or contemplate the universum ; or reproduce a certain selection from past ages, as that of the Homeric cycle, or the age of Pericles in Greece, or the Mediæval times ; — but these, while words of excellent counsel, and commending the selection of an excellent copy for imitation, have no elements of strength or freedom. They become the evidence of our own poverty and vacancy, and the absence of our own ideal. These pageants have an attraction for the eye, and we might act our parts well enough in them, and accumulate their theatrical properties, and hold the world as our stage for these mimic shows. But there would be no power in them, and we inherit even from these ages, more than the attractions of the eye. The life of the spirit is alone the condition of strength and freedom. This alone sustains man in his self-determination, toward the fulfillment of his own ideal. This alone lifts him above the external. This alone gives to man the real development, which apart from it may be traced only in the continuance of a type, that in a succession of conditions is subject to variations consequent upon those conditions, and is resolved in its termination into the attrition of molecular forces.

The Christ came, *in the fullness of time.* When S. John writes, *in the beginning was the Word,* the thought of man is not carried back through a mere numeration, or a series in numeration, and it is not referred to a merely vacant conception of being. In the process of logic, through finite conditions, the notion of being is an empty phase of thought, and is resolved through a logical necessity into mere nothingness; but the notion of being derived from finite conditions, is not to be applied to the being of God. The expression of the apostle carries the thought back to One who was in the beginning, and whose manifestation was in the fullness of time, and on whom the thought of man may rest. There were thence, through the historical life of the world, the courses in the process of time which moved in and toward the advent of the Christ, and the procession of the Holy Spirit.

The life of the spirit is not, then, subject to the law of necessity; it does not begin in the line of physical descent, nor terminate with the cessation of physical forms. The Christ says, *that which is born of the flesh is flesh; and that which is born of the Spirit is spirit.* S. Paul says, *flesh and blood cannot inherit the kingdom of God; neither doth corruption inherit incorruption.*

There is a line of evolution through physical forms, and there is also the procession of the Spirit: S. Paul says, *that was not first which is spiritual, but that which is physical; and afterward that which is spiritual. The first man is of the earth, earthy: the second man is the Lord from heaven.*

The words which henceforth become the new testament, and are to bear the witness of the life given for the world, are testamentary of an incorruptible inheritance: *I will put my law in their inward parts, and write it in their hearts; and will be their God, and they shall be my people, and they shall teach no more every man his brother, and every man his neighbor, saying, Know the Lord: for they shall all know me, from the least of them unto the greatest of them, saith the Lord; for I will forgive their iniquity, and I will remember their sin no more.* The words are verified, *I will pour out my spirit upon all flesh.* It is in man that the spirit has its dwelling. Man is the tabernacle. The body becomes the temple of the Holy Ghost. The words which represent the presence of the Spirit with man do not refer to a remote life. They are not the suggestion of some pale illusion, or some vague emotion. They speak of walking and of dwelling in the spirit.

The Christ, in his own life, manifested the life of the spirit. In his own life there was the presence and the inspiration of the spirit; *the Spirit descended upon him.* It is the witness to the oneness of his life, who came from the Father, with the life of humanity. It is the evidence of the presence of the Spirit with the Son of man. The Spirit which was with the Christ in the beginning of his work on the earth was with him until the close. The Christ, in the closing events of his life, was led by the spirit; *he through the eternal Spirit offered himself.*

The life of the spirit is not simply the indefinite life; — it is the determinate life. It is not simply the life which before was absent; but its precedent is in the life of the Christ, in the realization of the truth, and the fulfillment of righteousness in the life of humanity.

There is knowledge, but there is yet a wider knowledge open and opening unto men. There is no limit set for thought. The Christ says, *when the Spirit is come, he will guide you into all truth.*

There are many observances, customs, laws, institutions, but there are none that are to impose upon the life of the spirit. They are to become the evidence of it; they are to be formed in it. Their verification is to be unto the spirit. The value and measure of all forms is as they express and embody the life of the spirit. The law of all forms is in the words, *the sabbath was made for man, and not man for the sabbath.*

The Christ, the Word of God, manifests, in the spirit, that which was from the beginning: *in the beginning was the Word, and the Word was with God, and the Word was God.* The Word of God in the life of the spirit may go forth in human life, and in the events which become formative in human history. The Word of God is the informing power of the revelation of God in the finite world. The Word of God is not, by any figure, to be identified with a book, or a temple, or a minster, or a shrine; nor with one through whom, in books or temples, a message is brought to men: S. John says, *I fell down at his feet to worship the angel; and he said unto me, See thou do it not; I am thy fellow-servant and of thy brethren: worship God.*

The life of the spirit has its witness to the world in the Church.

The Church has an organic unity and life.

The Church is the company of all faithful people.

The Church has a form and order, in the fulfillment of the life of the spirit, and thence in the freedom of the spirit, in the historical courses of the world, and in consistence, in their divine institution, with the organic being and development of the family and the nation in the life of humanity.[1]

The Church is the witness to the life of the spirit in humanity. It is not the source of the life of the spirit, but the witness of it. The Spirit is not the gift of the church, but the church of the Spirit. The words of faith which cannot be transposed are, *I believe in the Holy Ghost; in the holy catholic Church.*

The Church is the witness to the redemption of the world. It is not in it alone that the necessity of the redemption is apparent, and it is not itself the object and end of the redemption,

---

[1] " That was the beginning of a society which could be nothing but universal, because it stood in the name of the Son of God and Son of man." (Maurice, *Sermons*, vol. i. p. 9.)

but it is the witness to the redemption of the world. It shows forth the divine sacrifice, the Lamb of God who taketh away the sins of the world.

The Church is the witness to the inspiration of the spirit. The life of the Church is in the presence of the spirit. It is the evidence and recognition, — the response in the life of humanity to the eternal Spirit, the communion of the spirit, in which the life of man has its eternal foundation and its unity and its peace.[1]

The Church is the witness to the being and continuance of the Christ in the world. It is built upon the person of the Christ, and is formed in relations with him. It is not founded upon abstractions. It does not rest upon a proposition or a system of propositions in the forms of thought. S. Paul writes of its communion as *built upon the foundation of the apostles and prophets, Jesus Christ himself being the chief corner stone, in whom ye also are builded together for an habitation of God through the Spirit.*

The Church is the witness to the life and the realization of the truth in the world. It is not

[1] " The Christ chooses the *Church* to be the witness of his love to mankind. The *sect* chooses Christ, because it is convinced that his doctrine is better than that of the founders of other religions; and then goes on to choose Cephas, or Paul, or Apollos, as having the most refined or satisfactory form of that doctrine. So the person of Christ becomes lost in certain opinions which the sects have taken up respecting him." (Maurice, *Sermons*, vol. iv. p. 9.)

alone the encouragement of a disposition toward the truth, nor the evidence of the recognition of the truth; it is that, but it is the testament of the realization of the truth in the world. It is to make manifest its light to the world. An apostle writes of the Church as *the pillar and ground of the truth*; and again, of its life in the Christ, S. Paul says, it is *his body, the fullness of him that filleth all in all.*

The holy catholic Church is the communion of saints. The life of the spirit is the life of communion with God. It is not a communion which is measured by finite limitations, and it is not distant in place nor remote in time. But the world is slow to receive. this, and is concerned with its own nothingness and emptiness. This communion is transposed; or is held as the association of an adjourned company. It is foisted into the future, in that conception in which the things not seen are still apprehended as some future temporality, and the present is occupied only with indefinite notions among its pure negations. This communion, by a sheer lift, is carried into another world, which is then only another world, in the succession to this world. The vague aspiration which wearies of its own vacancy, and the imagination which lingers among the things which are seen, the things of earth and time, brings to this its own detachments. The writer of the Epistle to the Hebrews says, *ye are come unto this com-*

munion. It is not *ye shall come to this communion.* That is the revision of the skepticism of
the world. The argument of the writer of the
epistle is to show that the Christ has rent asun-
der the veil which separates the earth from the
heavens, and those who are in the world from
those who have left it. It is not a communion
to which men are told that they shall come, nor
can the imagination pass beyond these words; *ye
are come unto the city of the living God, and to
an innumerable company of angels, to the general
assembly and church of the first-born, which are
written in heaven, and to God the Judge of all,
and to the spirits of just men made perfect.*
These words embrace the whole realization of that
historical life ; *ye are come unto Mount Zion, and
unto the heavenly Jerusalem, and unto Jesus, the
Mediator of the new covenant.*

The Church has preserved the writings called
the Old and the New Testament. This word has
itself a significant value as indicating their testamentary character. The Christ says of the writings of the Old Testament, *they are they which
testify of me.*

The Church has not preserved the original doc-
uments or instruments of these writings. It has
not preserved any manuscript of them, of the first
or second or third century. It has not preserved
the external evidence, in connection with them,

in verification of their contemporary transcription. It has not preserved all of them in a perfect form, and the only copies of some of them, now known to exist, are incomplete ; or appear as a fragment, as the closing pages of the Gospel of S. Mark. It has not preserved the verification of the individual authorship of some of them, and there may be no longer a verification of the name of the writer ; so that it is indifferent what name, if any, may be attached to them, — as the Epistle to the Hebrews. It has not preserved these writings from interpolations, which in some instances may certainly, and in some conjecturally appear, with the critical study and inquiry of scholars, in comparison of their variations, as the narrative of the woman taken in adultery, or the description of the three witnesses in the Epistle of S. John ; while yet the manuscripts in some instances, as the Gospel of S. Luke, although not without various readings, are yet of very considerable scriptory excellence.

The Church has read, indifferently with the original, an excellent translation : as, for instance, the translation into the Latin of S. Jerome, or the translation into the Gothic of Ulfilas, or the translation into the English of Wicliffe, or of the company of scholars of the sixteenth century. The writings of the Old Testament, when they are referred to by writers of the New Testament, are with citations from the recent and more common

version, in the translation of scholars in Alexan-
dria, called the Septuagint. These citations are
usually given in an illustrative way, and with indifference to literary precision.

The Church has held the verification of these
scriptures in the life of the spirit. It is in their
verification as *words that are spirit and truth,* —
the canon which alone the Christ has given. It is
their verification to the conscience and the consciousness of men. It is through their recognition, in the life of the spirit in humanity, in the
development through which the Word of God reveals itself in righteousness and judgment unto
men, that the Christ says, *heaven and earth may
pass away, but my words shall not pass away.*

The Bible, which is the simplest phrase of literature, the synonym of the Book, is the term
which comprehensively describes these writings.

The Bible is a book written in literal forms;
subject to the ordinary rules of construction, as
defined in the science of grammar.

The Bible is a book written in languages, as the
Hebraic, the Chaldaic, the Greek, or Græco-
Hebraic; subject to the ordinary rules of derivation and distinction, as defined in the science of
comparative philology.

The Bible is a book written in manuscripts;
which require in their transcription and authentication the critical study which belongs to the science, which, in comparing, for instance, the uncial

with other styles, is the science which deals with scriptory forms.

The Bible is a book which has been subject to the mutations of literature. It is written in manuscripts of unequal value, no one of which is entirely perfect in itself, so as to displace all others, and none are free from obscure or various readings. It has suffered simply the mutations of literature, and has had no exemption from them.

It embraces the most varied forms of literature ; as genealogies, laws, histories, records of legislative and judicial procedure, methods of sanitary, civil, and military administration. There is legend and myth ; there are various forms of poetry ; the ode, as in the antiphone of Moses and Miriam ; the drama, as in the Book of Job ; the idyl, as in the Song of Solomon ; the lyric, as in the book of the Psalms, and the opening pages of the Gospel of S. Luke ; and in the writings of S. Paul, citations from the Greek comedy, as from Menander.

These scriptures embraced, in substance, all the literature that the ancient Hebrew people possessed. Their productions in art and music always remained rude and simple, and in architecture they were the common adaptations of a primitive mode of life, or often the reproductions of forms copied from Egypt, or imported from Phœnicia.

There are traces in these writings of the races, countries, and ages in which they appeared, and of climatic conditions, with respect to languages and customs and laws. There is a popular element, as in the stories of Samson and Ruth; and there is also a priestly and a kingly element, as in the books of the Chronicles and Kings. In some books there are the traces of reflective phases of thought, as in the book of Ecclesiastes; and in some there are traces of Asiatic forms and Asiatic institutions.

These scriptures were written by various writers in various ages, and bear the note and accent of the individuality of these writers in their modes of expression. If it needs to be said, the literary forms of the older parts rise often to great dignity of expression, as the later chapters of Isaiah and the books of Hosea and Job; and they have, in this quality, a comparative excellence in the literature of the world. There is in the New Testament, not an indifference to literary form, but no distinction of literary form. These writings are simply narrative, in a biographical arrangement, or in the style of letters that are few and direct, and very unequal in their expression. There is a historical narrative of a discursive character, apparently embracing the work of various writers. The Epistle to the Hebrews has a singular finish, with an antithetic expression, and an elaborate detail of historical portraiture that indicates the culture of the writer in schools of rhetoric in his age. The evangel of S. Luke is commended for the diligence and thoroughness of its research.

The writings of S. Paul, in the epistles, which may be distinctively called catholic, indicate more plainly the modifications to which the Greek language was subject when it became the instrument for the expression of Hebrew forms of thought; and they indicate also, in their illustrative expression, the influence of a knowledge of Roman law in an age of great Roman lawyers. But the writings of S. Paul have no literary form to commend them, — to bring them into comparison, in Greek with the consummate beauty of phrase in Æschylus, or the repose in the style of Plato, or the sustained strength of the masterful style of Aristotle. There is often, from language of great elevation, a lapse to some digressive phrase; as, for an extreme instance, in the thirty-third verse of the fifteenth chapter of the first epistle to the Corinthians, which drops and moves on with a quotation from the Greek comedy. They lack the form which belongs to the great hymns of the Vedas, and the constructive unity and consonance with a formal system, which belongs to the Koran. The Koran is also better preserved, and has suffered less in transcription, with proportionately fewer obscure or various readings. The style has no distinctive quality; but they who, in common parlance with religious society, speak of their beautiful liturgy, suggest a comparison with the hymns of the Vedas; and they who write of the poetry of the Bible must draw their parallel with Æschy·

lus and Shakespeare, and the masters of the literary art to which they invite attention.

The Bible has a unity which is deeper than any structural form, however various and complete. This prevails with a continuous and continually increasing manifestation through the whole. It is not merely the unity which appears in the literature of a people, as the Latin or the English literature; it is that, but it is more and other than that. It is not merely the unity which attaches to the continuous history, the institutions, laws, customs, wars of a people; it is that, but it is more and other than that.

The Bible is the record of the revelation of God. It is the record of a revelation of God in man and to the world.[1] It is testamentary to the revelation of God to and through the world. This revelation, and not a literature nor a body of traditions, is the ground of the unity which it discovers. It is the record of the revelation of God

[1] The Church has no theory, it will have none, of the inspiration of books. A theory may be in the way of recognizing the facts. The words of the Church are, "*I believe in the Holy Ghost, the Lord and Giver of Life, who spake by the prophets.* It is an inspiration of men. The Bible speaks, as the proverb of the Talmud is, "in the tongue of the sons of men."

"The maxim of the whole book is that God is the educator of that people and of every people, that all circumstances are his instruments; that all events are assertions of his presence; that whatever happens to men is a means of showing to them his righteousness, and of moulding them to his image." (Maurice, *Sermons,* vol. i. p. 34.)

in his relation with humanity ; in the fulfillment of his eternal purpose, which was before the foundation of the world ; in the righteousness in which he manifests his own being, and in the life which he has given for the world. It is of the coming of his kingdom, in which the kingdoms of this world become the kingdoms of the Christ. It is of a revelation in an order in the world of the family and the nation. It is of a revelation of and in the Christ.

The sacraments of the Church are the witness to the will of God in its realization on this earth, and to the coming of the new life, the life of the spirit in the world. They are the witness to the real presence of the Christ with humanity, which he has redeemed.

The baptism is the regeneration of humanity in the coming of the spirit. It is the declaration of the true and eternal life of man. The holy communion is the manifestation of the perfect and finished sacrifice, in which alone there is the interpretation of the sacrifice and death of this earth. The sacraments compass the birth and death of man, in their eternal significance.

The sacraments become the evidence of the sacredness of the common life of humanity. They take up the types of nature in its own life. This water is the symbol of purity ; this bread and wine are the symbols of the strength and joy of man. They are the common elements of life. They are the witness of the presence of Him in the life of humanity, in whom the worship of the visible is overcome and destroyed. They bring their consecration to the family and the nation. This baptism is given to children of every tribe and race; as the sign of their common relation with Him, *who hath broken down the wall of partition, to make in himself of twain one new man.* It is given to children in their unconscious existence, as the evidence that the least and lowliest in this existence, is not separated from the Christ, but becomes a partaker in his redemption. These elements, — this bread and wine, — are the evidence that the daily life, the common life of this earth, may be transmuted. It is transmuted in union with him who died for the world.

The sacrament of the holy communion is not simply the memorial of a distant event, that is separated from us by tracts of time; and yet it has the strength and consolation of a sacred memory, as it testifies of a past that is glorified, and of the presence of Him in whom the past and the future are one.

The sacrament is not the setting forth of a sacrifice that requires to be perfected. It is the manifestation of the full, perfect, and sufficient sacrifice, which Christ made upon the cross for the sin of the whole world; but man may be made the partaker in this life, — the life that was given for the world.

The sacrament is the witness of that communion in which the limits of time and space, and the separations of death are overcome. It is with an unseen host; it is *with angels and archangels and all the company of heaven*. The sacrifice has been made once for all, but it is the ground of an eternal union. It has been made that men may be united with Him who has passed through death, who has entered within the veil, and who is presenting his finished sacrifice continually before the Father. It becomes the testament of a perpetually renewed life. This sacrifice the Church commemorates, and whatever theories we may devise, whatever forms and prescriptions of ritual we may observe, we cannot invest it with a character beyond that which it has in the words of S. Paul: *as often as ye eat this bread, and drink this cup, ye do shew the Lord's death till he come.* It is this alone, which gives its eternal significance to the death of every man, until he come. It bears us on toward the time when all the revelations and the sacraments of God shall close in the coming world, *the new heavens and new earth, wherein dwelleth righteousness.* The Church commemorates, therefore, with faith and hope, the one prevailing sacrifice, that its fulfillment may be in Him, beyond whose love there is no height, beneath whose love there is no depth.

The sacrament becomes the witness of an eternal life. It testifies of an eternal communion.

There is no symbol of union, in the life of humanity on this earth, that does not lend to it its
significance. In the mystic figure of S. John,
it is the ring and vesture of the bride; it is the
marriage supper of the Lamb. It is the invitation
of heaven; *Behold, I stand at the door and
knock: if any man hear my voice, and open the
door, I will come in to him, and will sup with him,
and he with me.* This is the simplest language,
and blends with human associations. It denotes
the fullest intercourse with Him who was alone on
this earth and suffered its necessities, with Him
who is with the hosts of heaven.

The sacraments become the witness of the character and end of the worship of the Church. They
set forth the object of worship, — the Will whose
manifestation is in the perfect love, from whom
sacrifice proceeds, and to whom it is given, and
with whom there is eternal life and communion.
It is the revelation through worship, of God the
Father and the Son and the Holy Ghost, with
whom we may become one in the life that is eternal. It is from the Father that the sacrifice proceeds, in the manifestation of the will of the Father.
The Christ said, *he that hath seen me hath seen the
Father.* The Church, in one of the greater ages
of its theological thought and life, distinctively
called S. John, the Divine; and if, in the theology
of S. John, there is the justification of this distinction, it is in the record of the words that por-

tray the conflict with formal notions of service, and formal notions of God; and the words which set forth the unity of God, the underground of the being and becoming of God in the world, the movement of the self-moved one, the manifestation of the perfect love.   S. John says, *Jesus answered and said unto them, Verily, verily, I say unto you, the Son can do nothing of himself, but what he seeth the Father do; for what things soever he doeth, these also doeth the Son likewise; for the Father loveth the Son, and sheweth him all things that himself doeth.*   Therefore in this worship, there is the rejection of the principality or power,—the will in heaven or earth, whose end is in self alone, the self-seeking will, and the recognition of the Will that is manifest in sacrifice, for the redemption and the realization of the eternal life of humanity.   This becomes the foundation of the worship of the family and the nation.   This worship sets forth the ground of the unity of all nations in the life of humanity.   We are enabled to offer the oblation of ourselves — the reasonable, holy, and living sacrifice, which brings us into communion with the will, which has offered the perfect oblation for the whole world.

The sacraments become then the witness of the presence of Him in whom is the eternal foundation of the family and the nation.   They give their interpretation to those events in which the unity **and** freedom of the nation is conserved.   The crises of judgment and deliverance in its history come to have a sacramental character. S. Paul writes to the church in Corinth of the sacramental character of events in the history of his own nation: *how that all our fathers were baptized in the cloud, and in the sea, and did all eat of the same spiritual meat, and did all drink of the same spiritual drink.* This is connected with the recital of historic incidents from age to age, of the most various circumstance. The sacraments are the evidence of the presence with the nation of the Lord of Hosts, from whom alone its deliverance proceeds, who is the leader of its armies, and alone the giver of victory.

The coming of the Spirit is in the assertion of the presence and coming of a principle or power of light in the world. This is not a vague illustration or an illusion of the imagination. There is the coming of an active power and an energy in the policies and politics of this earth, which they who build their dominations over it may refuse to recognize, but which they cannot always obstruct. This light discloses the false foundations, on which human society may aim to build, with its theories of property and art. This penetrates the utmost depths of sin, and the isolations of selfishness, and is in conflict with all the powers that dwell in its gloom, — the superstitions and the inquisitions and tyrannies of men. It will at last overthrow all repressive policies, which crush the spirits of men. The Christ says, *every one that doeth evil hateth the light, neither cometh to the light, lest his deeds should be reproved; but he that doeth truth cometh to the light.* The existence of this principle and this energy becomes the ground of strength and hope. Thus S. Paul says, *have no fellowship with the unfruitful works of darkness; all things that are convicted as wrong are shown to be what they actually are by light; for whatever shows things to be what they actually are is light. Wherefore he saith: Awake, thou that sleepest, and arise from the dead, and Christ shall give thee light.*

In the life of the spirit there is alone the ground of unity and reconciliation and peace. The finite is taken up and changed; — it is transmuted in the infinite. The struggle for existence becomes a conflict within man reaching to the depths of his nature, and then peace is not a mere quiescence, nor a balance of adverse forces, but it comes with unity and reconciliation. It has an ethical quality. It is the peace that the world cannot give. It is not derivative from the world; for in the physical process, from deep to deep; or in the organization of nature, from the germ to its decay; there is motion without cessation, and apparently it has its subsidence with the extinction of life, when the temperature has become uniform, as action exists in unequal conditions of heat and cold, which tend, though gradually, to their equalization. And life cannot be conceived in the physical process with the cessation of motion. There is the struggle for existence, but with no other rest, — only the rest of death. The Christ says, *my peace I give unto you; not as the world giveth give I unto you.* It is the peace which passeth understanding, for in it death is overcome; it is the peace of Him whose gift is eternal life; it is the peace of God.

There comes through the life of the spirit the knowledge and the realization of the truth. It is not simply the truth, apprehended as an inference from the observation of the physical process of the finite world, though it brings the elements of reflection and resolution to this knowledge. It is not truth simply as the formulas of science, but it is the truth that has a relation with the emotions and the will, and is the ground of their education. It is the truth that brings strength to love and freedom. It is the sanctification of the truth. It is formed in the relations and through the events of life, and not in separation from them. It is attained in and not apart from the family and the nation. It has its ground in the will of God: S. Paul says; *this is the will of God, even your sanctification.*

In the life of the spirit, the life of righteousness is to have its recompense. It has not that recompense for its end, and it is formed not for gain, — not for the hope of gaining heaven, and it has not thus an end external to itself. But it is the characteristic of a recent school of ethics that it should reject this, and leave it with mere negations. It may be, in an unbelieving age, when weariness and doubt seem to ally themselves with the corruption of the grave; when faith and hope become the mockery of the world; when trust in the love of God, as the central principle of the world, is made the jest of the school and the subject for the derision of the multitude in the popular assembly; it may be in that age that men are bidden to live with faith, *looking for a recompense.* The endurance that meets persecution for righteousness, has the promise of the beatific life; *rejoice and be exceeding glad, for great is your reward in heaven.* It is not the return of work and its obligation, for *it shall be given unto this last, even as unto thee;* it is not the wages of service, *the gift of God is eternal life.*

The life of the spirit is the new life. It is the life of the regeneration. It is the life that is not determined in finite conditions, as in the physical process, but it is the real, the eternal life. The Christ asserts the necessity of this regeneration, not because of antecedent conditions of sin; but because, *that which is born of the flesh is flesh, ana that which is born of the Spirit is spirit.*

This regenerative power is manifest in the lives of men and nations. It goes forth to the baptism of all nations. The regeneration is a life that is not the sequence nor continuance of physical forces, nor determined by physical contingencies, nor having its conclusion in the dissolution of physical forms. It is not the life that is *after the traditions of men or the rudiments of the world.* It is the true life of humanity, the life that it has in the Christ, the real head of the human race; *the first Adam is of the earth earthy : the second Adam is the Lord from heaven.*

The process and end of the life of the spirit is the development of a perfect humanity. The aim is the attainment and fulfillment of a perfect manhood. The Christ says, *be ye perfect, even as your Father in heaven is perfect.* It is the law and fulfillment of a perfect and perfected humanity. If a man aims to be more or other than a man, then he must become less than a man. But this is not simply the development of a life in identity with nature ; it is not simply the projection of this physical being, but while there is in it the extinction of none of its powers or its energies, it is a life formed and determined through the mediation of the spirit. In this process nature is controlled and determined through the mediation of the spirit, and it is this and this alone that gives its significance to the ideal of art.

It is the realization of a perfect manhood. For this end the Son of God became the Son of man. S. Paul says its end is that *we all come in the unity of the faith, and of the knowledge of the Son of God, unto a perfect man, unto the measure of the stature of the fullness of Christ.* It is a perfect humanity. This does not yield to age, with its increase of infirmities. Its process is not from life unto death. It does not grow old with the waning of the years. S. Paul says, *though our outward man perish, yet the inward man is renewed day by day.*

While the process and end of the life of the Spirit is the development of a perfect humanity this is not through a principle of exclusion, but there is the negation and transmutation of a principle of exclusion, and its end is in the realization of a perfect human society.[1] In the manifestation of the Son of man, there is the ground of the redemptive life of humanity. It is the manifestation of the foundation of the life of humanity in the fatherhood of God and the brotherhood of man. It is of and in the

---

[1] " The apostles did not dare — they did not find it possible — to think of human society, except as constituted in Christ. It was the confusion, the unbelief of men, to regard themselves as capable of fellowship and of existence without him. It was theirs to proclaim that there could have been no families, no nations, to resist the selfish tendencies which each of us is conscious of in himself, and complains of in his neighbors, if there had not been one living centre of the whole body of humanity, one head of every man." (Maurice, *Sermons*, vol. iv. p. 10.)

Christ, who has brought to man in his own life the law of love and sacrifice. It affirms the principle that *no man liveth and no man dieth to himself.* It sets forth the organic relations of human society.[1] The law is coming to be recognized, which not only regards society as a body, but affirms that none can be isolated from its relations, *whether one member suffer, all the members suffer with it.* It is alone in righteousness and freedom that there is laid the ground of the enduring order and development of human society. The law of the Christ becomes the law of humanity: *bear ye one another's burdens, and so fulfill the law of Christ.* The bond of society is in the truth, *wherefore putting away lying, speak every man truth with his neighbor, for we are members one*

[1] " The name of the God of Abraham and of Isaac is not lost in the name of the Father and the Son and the Holy Ghost ; the perfect and universal revelation explains all the gradual discoveries that are leading to it. And that perfect revelation will be proved at last to be what an ecclesiastical system, what philosophical liberalism has tried to be and failed,— the assertion of a humanity in which all races are equally partakers. The Church which is to be, will not be another than that which has grown up under authority of this commission, and has stood ever since in different lands, in different degrees of strength and feebleness, of sincerity and corruption. She will only have learned through hard suffering the foundation which she has forgotten. She will be purged of whatever loveth and maketh a lie, that she may understand she is the witness of truth to all nations." (Maurice, *Sermons*, vol. iv. p. 48.)

" A deliverance from lies would be the great deliverance for us all. Nor may we obtain it, nor society be brave and truthful, nor we, the members of society, be so until we take S. Paul's words in their full sense: *Wherefore, putting away lying, speak every man truth of another.* It is the law of Christ that becomes the ground of the development of domestic and national economies in human society.

The election of humanity is in the Christ, in the fulfillment of the purpose that was the eternal purpose of God before the foundation of the world.[1] It is not the separation of some from the human race by a process of inclusion, and the rejection of others by the same process, from a life of righteousness. It is the manifestation of the will of God, revealed in the Christ, toward all men, in the manifestation of the perfect life. S. Paul writes of *the faith of God's elect, which God, that cannot lie, in hope of eternal life, promised before the world began.* This election is in the will of God, and is manifest in the continuous course of the world. It is the election of all men. It is not the selection of some for happiness and some for misery. S. Paul could write of the condition of his own nation when he went to the na-

with his neighbor, for we are members one of another. There is the secret. We do not believe that we are members one of another. We do not believe that there is one living and true head of us all. We do not think that he knows our secrets, and wishes us to be true in our inward parts, and is himself the truth. This — the vice of the beggar and the opulent, of him who sells votes and him who buys them — can only be extirpated by faith in one who ascended on high, and united us all to God, and to each other." (Maurice, *Sermons*, vol. vi. p. 85.)

[1] "Jesus is the one elect; and those who, by taking part with him, become members of his body, become also members of the election; and those who continue to resist him shut themselves out from the election." (Erskine, *Memoirs*, p. 228.)

tions, *until the fullness of the Gentiles be come in, and so all Israel shall be saved.* And the nations which come into existence in the course of the Christian history, while they rest in the same will, and are led through the same redemption, go forth in the realization of a more perfect unity and toward a more perfect freedom.

There is in the life of the spirit the revelation of the source and end of life in its eternal relations. The words of faith are of *the Holy Ghost, the Lord and Giver of Life.* The representation of human life, which has thence its ground, is of an eternal life, which was promised before the world was, and subsists in infinite relations, with the Father, and the Son, and the Holy Ghost. This representation is imperfectly expressed in the words, — the education of the world. The representation, also, of life merely as a probation,— if in that notion it is assumed that men are subjected to a system of tests, as coins are weighed on well-adjusted scales; or that each, here or hereafter, has one or several fair chances in a method of indifference, in which the result is a subject of divine conjecture, so far as the chances go,— this representation does not consist with the facts of human life, nor with the revelation of the Christ. It does not consist with the relative duration of existence, nor with the relative ignorance and incapacity of tribes and races. The phrase which allows to each, at some period, a fair chance, has the same superficial ground and false conception of life. If the chances of Tyre and Sidon were fair, those of Sodom and Gomorrah were less than fair. But this phrase does not consist with the simplest representation of the revelation of the Christ, with the election and grace of God, with the love manifested in the Son of God who became the Son of man.[1] It does not consist with a true conception of the freedom of the will, which certainly involves the power of choice; but freedom is more and other than that. The phrase which represents life as a discipline, and an education into the knowledge and love and freedom of God, is consistent more nearly with the revelation of God. It is a life in the limitations of the finite,

[1] " There are few religious phrases that have had such a power of darkening men's minds as to their true relation to God, as the common phrase that we are here in a state of probation, under trial, as it were. We are not in a state of probation, we are in a process of education, directed by that eternal purpose of love which brought us into being. When we apprehend that we are in a process of education, that God will carry to its fulfillment, however long it may take, we feel that the loving purpose of the Father is over us, and that the events of life are not appointed as testing us, whether we will choose God's will or not, but real lessons into training us to make the right choice.

" The gospel declares that not inevitable laws, however great, however righteous, but a being of righteousness and love, guides and rules the universe, and that his own purpose in creating and sustaining man is to make him a partaker in his own blessedness by making him a partaker in his own righteousness, and that all the events of life constitute the education by which he would train us and lead us to that end." (Erskine, *Memoirs*, p. 376.)

that compasses them in the life that is infinite. It is the endurance of all that life brings, and through endurance there is victory; it is *the kingdom and patience of Jesus Christ.* It follows him who *learned obedience by the things which he suffered ; and, being perfected, became the author of eternal salvation to all who obey him.* It is on this earth the discipline of virtue that in its necessary conditions, becomes the incontrovertible argument and evidence of a life that is not determined in the process of the physical world ; it verifies the words which were the strength of our fathers, and shall be the strength of manhood until the end of time : *he that hath suffered in the flesh hath ceased from sin.* This life is a growth, and, through the redemption of the Christ, into the life of Go1. It is through the finite into a life which has its foundation in the eternal life, its freedom in the infinite life. It is a growth in a life which is self-determined, and is not determined by external limitations. It is not the subjection of being to another, for it is immoral that one should be used as a means for an end external to his own being, or to subserve the being of another to himself. It is the development of being in its own whole. The Christ says, *No man taketh my life from me. I lay it down of myself. I have power to lay it down and I have power to take it again.*

In the life of the spirit, through the courses of

history, the ritual of the Church is to be formed in the law and unity and freedom of the spirit. Its ritual is formed in the requirement, *they that worship the Father shall worship him in spirit and in truth.* Its unity is in the Spirit. It does not assume the subjection of the spirit to the letter, nor to the precedent of those who sit in the seats of the elders. Its end is universal. It does not look for the perpetuation of Jerusalem, nor of Athens or Rome, with their separate sanctities.[1] We have no continuing city here: *we are come to the heavenly Jerusalem.* We are bidden to journey toward no earthly town or city, however great in the historical courses of the world, and however many the attractions be that are recounted of it: *the Jerusalem which is above is free, which is the mother of us all.*

The life of the spirit is the eternal life of man. It is not spatial nor temporal; it is not bounded by these coasts of time; it is here and now, but it is not at this place to be described by the location of this place, and it is not at this time to be measured by the termination of this time. It is not in the past, and it is not to be foisted away into the future; *he that believeth hath eternal life.*

---

[1] The only law of ritual affirmed in the First General Council of the Church, Nicæa, A. D. 325, is Canon XX. This commends the posture of standing in prayer, which it seems good to the holy synod to prefer. But it does not follow that a law of ritual of this character is necessarily to be held as permanent.

There is in man the suspect that in the transient course of things there is yet an intimation of that which is not transient. The grass that fades has yet in the folded and falling leaves of its flower that perishes the intimation of a beauty that does not fade. The treasures that are frayed by the moth and worn by the rust are not as those in which love and faith and hope abide. There is a will·that in its purpose does not yield to mortal wrong. There is a joy that is not of emulation. There is a freedom that is other than the mere struggle for existence in physical relations, and is not determined in its source or end by these finite conditions.

This is the life of the spirit. It is born of God; it is of the uncreated Spirit; it is begotten, not made; it proceeds from the Father and the Son; it is in *the fellowship of the Holy Ghost.*

The inspiration of the Spirit, the Christ recognized; the Spirit descended upon him and was sent from him. It is the evidence of a relation and a communion manifested in the Christ with the life of man. The prophetic and the priestly and the kingly line closed in the Christ; — only as from him there was to come the prophetic and priestly and kingly powers of humanity.

There is in men and in nations the consciousness of the existence of physical and of spiritual powers and relations. It is not·that the life of man is

wholly physical until a certain epoch, and there-
after wholly spiritual ; although in the racial development of man, the physical precedes the spiritual.   There is thence the ethical conflict, in which
the spiritual comes to be apprehended as before and
above the physical, and striving toward its realization.   This has its illustration in the widest ranges
of literature and art.   This is the ground of those
words of counsel, *walk in the Spirit, and ye shall
not fulfill the lust of the flesh, for the flesh lust-
eth against the spirit, and the spirit against the
flesh.*

The life of the spirit has its fulfillment in the
life of humanity in God.   It is the fulfillment of
the will that held its purpose in love before the
world was.   It is the love that is stronger than
death, and in its perfect fulfillment man is brought
into oneness with God.   S. John says, *God is love,*
and *he that loveth is born of God.*

Thus the phrase, the last judgment, is not distinctively characteristic of the revelation of the
Christ.   The judgment is continuous, and in the
increasing realization of righteousness and truth
and love.   It is not, as an ultimate event, — the
final goal of humanity, and the end of all things.
S. Paul says, *then cometh the end, when God shall
be all in all.*

The judgment, in the separation and discrimination in the divine light, of the eternal signifi

cance of good and evil, and their consequence in eternal life and eternal death, becomes the ground of an infinite hope. It is faith and hope and love that abide. But the greater is love. This love that was before the world was, does not perish with the perishing world. It will follow every child of time, and it does not yield to death.

The assumption that the doom of each and all, in the moment of physical death, is irrevocably fixed, is the assumption of the extremest fatalism. From the finite conceptions of men, it derives its moulds and measures for the divine love, and in the courses of human thought it is formed on pessimism in alliance with dualism. It places a finite limit to the divine redemption. It is an ultimate subjection to sin and death. That the moral degradation of men and of nations tends toward it, is no evidence that no other and higher powers shall prevail toward their perfect fulfillment. The Christ has conquered death, and in death there is no limit to his power. The law and life which the Christ has manifested is the universal law and life, and there is no place that can be detached from it, in the universe.

The relation of every man to humanity in the Christ is the ground of the faith and hope and love which justify the words, that bid men to count not the ninety and nine, but to seek with unceasing quest for one that is lost.

We are to strive in a world where infinite good

and evil are, and we can only overcome evil with good. That humanity is joined in the bonds of that love which was before the foundation of the world, and that virtue is brought into an active conflict with evil, is the assurance of their ultimate triumph. It is not immediate, and vice and crime may still go on; *he that is unjust shall be unjust still.* But the ultimate realization of the divine redemption shall be in the overthrow of every power that has held the spirit of man in subjection, and wrought its degradation. But the consequences of evil continue through an ethical development. We may be saved from sin and hell; we may be lost in their vacancy and misery and despair, and suffer their confinement. Gehenna was not far from Jerusalem, and its fires were still burning, when it became the type of the consequences of sin for man. This gives intenser significance to the fire that is not quenched, in the judgment of the wicked.

The fulfillment of the redemption is the realization of righteousness, the fulfillment in humanity of the righteousness of the Son of God, who became the Son of man. It is the victory of faith, but this is not for the individual alone and within his own spirit. It is not a victory that separates him from humanity, nor withdraws him from the world that has been redeemed, but it brings out the ground of his relation to humanity. It is faith in One, who being the Son of God has become the Son of man.

But the thoughts of men in the revelation of God through the Christ, and in the life of the spirit, are not sent forth to wander in vacuity. The family and the nation are not to be regarded as insubstantial in their unity and foundation. The precedent of their life is not to be found only in the vestiges that are left, as the strata of geological deposits, to indicate the succeeding tribes and races that have passed over a continent, one vanishing before another, as if worn out in the struggle.

The records of the Old Testament have no assertion of the immortality of the soul, as it is apprehended in the religions and the philosophies of the world. But there is the assurance that the family and the nation are immortal. The suggestion of a life that is immortal is in the hope that rests in the continuous life of the family and the nation, which have their unity and foundation in God. This is the hope that came to the king of Israel, that each may live since they live.

The records of the New Testament have not the assertion of the immortality of the soul, as subsequent to the incident of physical death, primarily for their subject. It is the life of humanity in the Christ that is the evidence of the incorruptible, the immortal life. The Christ has brought to the spirit of man the realization of life and immortality; *he has brought life and immortality to light.*

This is the life of the spirit, the real life, in which alone there is the satisfaction of the spirit. This is the life that shall not see corruption. It does not decompose with the physical elements, nor suffer their decay. It is not measured by the ashes of the urn, nor by the confines of the grave. The strength that moves with its forces is that of an eternal life. The power that animates it is the power that is not of the sequences of earth and time; it is *the power of the resurrection.*

The resurrection from the dead is in and through the Christ. The Christ has overcome death; *death hath no more dominion over him.*[1]

The resurrection is not the resurrection of the physical body. It is not the resultant of the law of physical necessity, nor subject to physical conditions. It is not the recovery and reconstruction

---

[1] "*Death hath no more dominion over him; for in that he died, he died unto sin once; in that he liveth, he liveth unto God.* The apostle presents the fact of the resurrection as a manifestation of the divine relation in which Christ stood to the Eternal Father; of the divine life which dwelt in him because he was the Son of God; of the divine energy which was every hour sustaining that life, and which in weakness, agony, on the cross, in the sepulchre, sustained it still." (Maurice, *Sermons*, vol. iv. p. 4.)

"This death, — this common death, — the death of him who died for all, is that in the likeness of which we are planted; here is the bond of perfect human fellowship; here is the assurance that death cannot break the bonds which hold us to each other, because the Love which established them had in death proved itself to be stronger than death." (Maurice, *Sermons*, vol. iv. p. 220.)

of the physical body from the physical elements. It is the resurrection of the spiritual body. The apostle says, *it is sown a physical body, it is raised a spiritual body: there is a physical body and there is a spiritual body.*

The resurrection is not in the evolution of the physical process of the world. That which is first is physical, and then that which is spiritual. But the spiritual has not its ground in nor its derivation from the physical. The end of the physical process for individuals and races is death. In this physical process and conclusion, as it is open to observation and its resultant knowledge, men become, and invariably, mere carrion that may be reduced to ashes or concealed beneath the sod, at last only to make other growths more rank. It is weakness to evade the invariable result which is thus within the observation and the resultant knowledge of men. S. Paul recognizes it with a clearness that is not exceeded by the writers of the physical school in their most recent literature; *corruption does not inherit incorruption.* This death is not averted by the strength of youth, nor the gift of wealth, nor the charm of beauty, nor the valor of armies. It is not overcome by the skill of those arts in which men are trained. But men recognize the weakness with which they yield to disease, and the advance of age, and the subjection to the law of death, and the dishonor of the grave, in this process of physical necessity.

The apostle says, *it is sown in corruption; it is raised in incorruption: it is sown in dishonor; it is raised in glory: it is sown in weakness; it is raised in power.* It was not necessary that the writers of the physical school should repeat the induction of the physical process in the observation and apprehension of life within the limits of the physical process. The apostle says, *flesh and blood cannot inherit the kingdom of God.* But there is, again, the assertion of another than this physical sequence; *this corruptible must put on incorruption, and this mortal put on immortality. So when this corruptible shall have put on incorruption, and this mortal shall have put on immortality, then shall be brought to pass the saying that is written, death is swallowed up in victory.*

The resurrection is not from a state which is subsequent to death, nor from a state which is separated by long intervals from death. It is not from a state that is intermediate between certain other states. It is the resurrection of the dead. It has that immediacy.[1]

[1] " After this life comes the fruition of his glory. The longing for selfish prizes has ceased ; the earthly weakness of desiring to exchange faith for sense has been taken away. What remains is the vision of that light which fills earth and heaven ; the revelation to the inward eye of God himself, as the eye of the spiritual body will, by degrees, become capable of taking in all the beauty and harmony of God's works. Yes! there is in all of us a sighing for home, a longing which nothing but the beholding of God can satisfy." (Maurice, *Sermons*, vol. iv. p. 126.)

This opens for men the communion of saints, which is involved in the life of the Church. They, who have gone, have not therefore passed into a condition of lethargy or vacancy. They may be nearer to us, as they are nearer to the perfect love. They may guide us toward a holier and ampler freedom, since they suffer no more the limitations of time. The veil is rent. There is with us the presence of the unseen host. It is not alone their memory that remains, their spirit may be with us. This brings to us the chastity of hope, *he that hath this hope in him purifieth himself.* It becomes the incentive to effort, *seeing we also are compassed about with so great a cloud of witnesses, let us lay aside every weight, and the sin which doth so easily beset us, and let us run with patience the race that is set before us.*[1]

---

[1] This communion, this presence of an unseen company, is recognized in the critical days, and recalled in the high services of nations. " It is not unnatural to feel that they who, by wisdom, by valor, by sacrifice, have contributed to maintain and perfect the institutions which we possess have also an interest in this day. To a spirit alive with memories of the time, and rejoicing in its presage of noble futures, recalling the great, the beloved, the heroic, who have labored and joyfully died for its coming, it will not seem too fond an enthusiasm to feel that the air is quick with shapes we cannot see, and glows with faces whose light serene we may not catch." (Storrs, *Oration*, July 4, 1876.)

There are memories in the life of a nation which find expression in very eloquent words, that move men with their truth, as no phrases of rhetoric could move them. At the meeting of the armies of the Nation at Chicago, June, 1880, it was said of a great soldier, " From the front of the ranks, and with his face to the foe, booted and spurred, he went into the presence of the God of Battles." (Gov-

It was the doctrine of the Pharisees that we shall rise at the last day. To them the Christ says, *the God of Abraham and the God of Isaac and the God of Jacob is not a God of the dead, but of the living, for all live unto him.* To those who said to him, in the expression of the popular thought, of one that was dead, "He shall rise again at the last day," he answered, *I am the resurrection and the life.* Through the resurrection the conception of death is itself changed. Death is no more clothed with the signs of victory over man.

Cullom, *Oration.*) But as the school of physical science concludes, did he go to the mingling of the physical elements, to the presence of a vaporous mist, only to add some more to that vaporous mist, or to the combination of molecular forces tending to the cessation of motion with the equivalence of temperatures? This name, *the God of Battles*, is very old; we have received it from our fathers, and it had a certain significance in a book which we have received, in the assertion of the presence of God, who is the leader of the armies of earth, and the only giver of victory. We may believe that he went into the very presence of Him whom he had followed, and that Host is with the nation always.

It was said, again, " They fought to keep our country on the map of the earth, and our flag in heaven." (Col. Ingersoll, *Oration.*) But if we accept the counsel of S. Paul, *Let your citizenship be in heaven*, we may believe that this is no vacant phrase, that it is very real ; that the flag is stirred, as it is borne to battle and sacrifice by diviner airs than those of earth, and is the witness of that divine life that is with the nation always.

Again it was said, "With a nobler ambition than the gaining of empire, they bore their puissant arms for the kingdom of man, where liberty reigneth forever." (Col. Vilas, *Oration.*) But we may believe that this *kingdom of the Son of man* is very real and has eternal foundations, and that the freedom of man is beyond the accident of earth in its perfect realization.

The term, — the immortality of the soul, — consists more strictly with the speculations of the schools of philosophy. It is a dry and abstract phrase. It is not a term which corresponds with those terms which are indicative of the revelation of the Christ, while yet it affirms a truth which has its fullest realization in this revelation. It is the affirmation of the spiritual life, which is immortal. This does not suffer corruption, nor yield to death. It is the life which is eternal: *the first man is of the earth earthy; the second man is the Lord from heaven: as we have borne the image of the earthy, we shall also bear the image of the heavenly.*

The apostle says, *the Christ was declared to be the Son of God by the resurrection from the dead.* He was, in the deepest significance of these words, the Son of man, the child of earth and time, and he suffered the incident of the life of earth, in these finite limitations, and became subject unto death; but his life had not its consummation in this physical process, as the resurrection was not a power which had its derivation from the physical process. If death seemed the negation of the physical process, there was in the resurrection the negation of death. But it was not the continuance of the finite; it was the perfect restoration and fulfillment of the finite in the coming of the life that was infinite. It lifts the faith and hope of man to God; the apostle says, *God raised Christ from the dead, and gave him glory that our faith and hope might be in God.*[1]

The faith of the resurrection, therefore, must always come with associations of joy. It is the conquest of life. The final victory is not with death. For the love that is stronger than death leads faith to look through death. Whatever be the confusion and variance of the world, and however widely misery prevail on the earth, the Church will strive to celebrate its service of the resurrection, with a joy imperfectly expressed in the opening flowers of spring, and by the exultant anthems that rise beyond the fanfare of trumpets and are borne from choir to choir.

The last enemy is destroyed and the conquest of humanity is complete. The apostle says, *the last enemy shall be destroyed, which is death.* There is no limit to these words, *as in Adam all die, even so in Christ shall all be made alive, but every man in his own order.*

The power of love and sacrifice is proven to be the mightiest power on earth. It is the power of him who was the first and is the last, who was in the beginning and is the end. It is the Lamb

---

[1] " S. Paul not only speaks of our Lord being made like unto us, but of our being made in his likeness. He does not limit this mode of expression, telling us that we may be made holy like Christ here, or glorious like Christ hereafter. He speaks of our death being cast in the mould of his death; of his being the only standard by which we can measure, the only type by which we can understand our own." (Maurice, *Sermons,* vol. ii. p. 218.)

that was slain from the foundation of the world, but it has become the sign of conquest as the cross has been borne in front of the armies of earth, borne on from the Church militant to the Church triumphant. In the vision of S. John the universality passes beyond our conception, *and every creature which is in heaven and on the earth and under the earth, and such as are in the sea, and all that are in them heard I saying, blessing and honor and glory and power unto him that sitteth upon the throne, and unto the Lamb forever and ever.*[1]

The subjection of all things is perfect, that God may be all in all. There is no fear of the end; perfect love has cast out fear. There is no fear of that which lies as the unknown, for the law which determines it is known. There is no fear of that which may be summoned forth from beyond the

---

[1] "When we speak of death, the resurrection, and the ascension, of the descent of the Holy Spirit, of the revelation of Christ as the judge of the quick and the dead, we are transported into a region to which our measures are inapplicable. *He has overcome death, he has taken away sin, he has led captivity captive.*" (Maurice, *Sermons*, vol. v. p. 43.)

"We receive, then, the message of redemption by the cross, of Christ's victory over the grave, as he and his apostles delivered it. The cross becomes far more than ever the sign in which, and in which alone, we hope to conquer, when we have acknowledged the Lamb in the midst of the throne. The resurrection becomes far more than ever the strength to the dying man, when the voice rings through all creation, *I am he that liveth and was dead; and, behold, I live forevermore, and have the keys of death and of hell.*" (Maurice, *Sermons*, vol. vi. p. 89.)

confines of this earth, nor drawn from the lowest deeps; for the same organic law prevails through all worlds, — the law manifested in the Christ, in his redemptive kingdom. There is, then, no power that is not brought into subjection to man, — no power in life or in death, in things present or things to come. There is no finite limitation to the redemption of the Christ, *whose kingdom shall have no end.* S. Paul says, the Christ being raised from the dead *is far above all principality and power, and might and dominion, and every name that is named, not only in this world but also in that which is to come.* The message of the worlds to come, of their law and power, is that the Christ is there, *Jesus Christ, the same yesterday, and to-day, and forever.*

The fulfillment of the life of humanity in the world is in the Christ in God. The end is not another world. The end is the perfect and perfected world. And the life of man is not to be for ever on and on, to overcome and still to overcome, to mark its advance by its journey from mile to mile, and by its transfer from field to field. That is the contingent of finite relations. The end is in the consummation of life, *the fullness of Him that filleth all in all.* There is no more the suffering and travail of earth. The love that was manifested in sacrifice has its fulfillment in the joy of the Redeemer. The apostle says, *Christ being raised from the dead, dieth no more.*

The death and the resurrection of the Christ are always to be connected with the ascension. This is the witness that no limits of time or space can separate the Christ from the world which he has redeemed. It is the witness of the presence of one who says *I am with you alway.*[1] It is the witness that the heavens are opened, and that their life becomes henceforth one with the life of earth. It becomes the incentive to duty in a life of faith and hope ; the apostle says, *if ye then be risen with Christ, seek those things which are above.* It is the evidence of a pure and redeemed and glorified humanity. It fulfills the transfiguration in the eternal glory of the Son of man. It

---

[1] "The faith which rests upon the death and the resurrection of Christ, without taking any account of his ascension, may serve as long as our thoughts are occupied chiefly with the condition of our own souls, and with the question how they may be saved here or hereafter. But when we are brought to feel, by one discipline or another, that we are bound up for good or for evil with our race, that we are not and cannot be exempt from any of its transgressions, then comes a demand for something more than the gift of pardon, than the promise of a better world, if we be worthy. When we are brought to this border land between despair and a hope that is beyond all that we can ask or think, the ascension day breaks in upon us, as with the light of seven suns. He has gone up on high. He is there, where our eyes cannot follow him, with the God who is and was and is to come, his Father and our Father. He is there, not separated by space from those whose nature he bears ; not separated from them in any sympathy; in all things what he was when he bore their infirmities, was made sin for them, died their death. And that which constitutes his perfect Humanity, his truth, his justice, his purity, his sympathy, — this is our inheritance." (Maurice, *Sermons*, vol. vi. p. 84.)

verifies the words of prophecy, *henceforth ye shall see the heavens opened, and the Son of man at the right hand of God.*

There is therefore for those who remain in the continuing life of earth no anticipation of things to come, such as is drawn in the conceptions of religion, as they are projected into the future, in the imagination of the world. The revelation that is to come is one with that that now is. After this life there shall come the beatific vision. The semblances of earth and time have gone. There is the manifestation to the spiritual eye of the fullness of the eternal glory. But there is no thought of the life to come that is apart from Him who on this earth *was parted from those who followed him, and carried up into heaven.* The voice that comes to those who remain is in the words, *thou canst not follow me now, but thou shalt follow me hereafter.* S. John says, *now are we the sons of God; and it doth not yet appear what we shall be; but we know that when he shall appear we shall be like him; for we shall see him as he is.*

The assumption that this course of human life is strictly the probation of the individual in his mature development, and that the terminus of this probation is in the incident of the death of the individual, and that the location of heaven and hell is beyond the earth, and that the object of salvation is transportation to the one and escape from the other, and that human life is evil, and that the few who have a conscious faith, which has yet in itself no ethical ground, are alone saved in the ultimate assize, to which all are summoned; — this is the staple of the various religions of the world.

The Christ has broken down the barriers of the grave. He has overcome death. He has opened the kingdom of heaven, that the earth and the heavens may become thenceforth one in their life. The superstitions which have divided and enslaved humanity, and the systems which have held on to a root of evil that was deeper than the love of God, are broken and thrown away. It is the day of deliverance. The will of God is manifested in love. The power of God is the power of the resurrection. In the victory of the Christ for humanity, there is the conquest of hell and of death; *he hath the keys of hell and of death.*

This is the deliverance of man from all the powers that have claimed dominion over him, and separated him from God. It is the freedom, in its perfect realization, of the redemptive power of the Christ of man. The grave has then no victory in its corruption. It is the perfect life, the life of those who have loved righteousness. It is the life of those who have cast off the garments of their own vanity and selfishness, and entered into the life of Him who is the Redeemer of the world.

It is the new life, the life of the fulfillment of the spirit; it is the life of humanity; and no man can claim it in his severance, but in the life of humanity in the Christ.

It fulfills the hope of man; it is beyond all that was prefigured in the prophetic soul of the wide world. It is the fulfillment of the Will, in the expression of the apostle, of *the God of hope.* It completes the vision of the days when the servant shall be as the master, and the bond shall be free. It is the time when the earth shall no more conceal her blood, nor cover her slain. It is the time, *when there shall be no more crying, neither shall there be any more pain, for former things are passed away.* It is *the new heavens and new earth, wherein dwelleth righteousness.*

When the apostle to the nations would express the life that is given in the revelation of God to the world, he says, *The grace of our Lord Jesus Christ, and the love of God, and the fellowship of the Holy Ghost be with us all evermore.*

I believe in one God the Father Almighty, Maker of heaven and earth, And of all things visible and invisible:

And in one Lord Jesus Christ, the only-begotten Son of God, Begotten of his Father before all worlds, God of God, Light of Light, very God of very God, Begotten, not made, Being of one substance with the Father, By whom all things were made; Who, for us men, and for our salvation, came down from heaven, And was incarnate by the Holy Ghost of the Virgin Mary, And was made man, And was crucified also for us under Pontius Pilate. He suffered, and was buried; And the third day he rose again, according to the Scriptures; And ascended into heaven, And sitteth on the right hand of the Father; And he shall come again with glory to judge both the quick and the dead, Whose kingdom shall have no end.

And I believe in the Holy Ghost, the Lord and Giver of Life; Who proceedeth from the Father and the Son, Who with the Father and the Son together is worshipped and glorified, Who spake by the Prophets; And I believe one Catholic and Apostolic Church; I acknowledge one Baptism for the remission of sins; And I look for the Resurrection of the dead; And the Life of the world to come. Amen.

A. D. 381–1881.